★★★★★★★★★★★ HARCOURT HORIZONS

States and Regions

Activity Book

Teacher's Edition

**Harcourt**

Orlando   Austin   Chicago   New York   Toronto   London   San Diego

Visit *The Learning Site!*
www.harcourtschool.com

Printed in the United States of America

ISBN 0-15-322607-2

1 2 3 4 5 6 7 8 9 10 073 10 09 08 07 06 05 04 03 02

The activities in this book reinforce social studies concepts and skills in **Harcourt Horizons: States and Regions.** There is one activity for every lesson and skill in the Pupil Edition. Copies of the activity pages appear with answers in the Teacher's Edition. In addition to activities, this book also contains reproductions of the graphic organizers that appear in the chapter reviews in the Pupil Edition. Multiple-choice test preparation pages for student practice are also provided. A blank multiple-choice answer sheet can be found after these content pages.

Contents

Introduction

·UNIT·

1

Chapter 1

Chapter 2

·UNIT·

2

Chapter 3

Name _____   Date _____

Multiple-Choice
Answer Sheet

Number your answers to match the questions on the test preparation page.

—— Ⓐ Ⓑ Ⓒ Ⓓ	—— Ⓐ Ⓑ Ⓒ Ⓓ	—— Ⓐ Ⓑ Ⓒ Ⓓ
—— Ⓕ Ⓖ Ⓗ Ⓙ	—— Ⓕ Ⓖ Ⓗ Ⓙ	—— Ⓕ Ⓖ Ⓗ Ⓙ
—— Ⓐ Ⓑ Ⓒ Ⓓ	—— Ⓐ Ⓑ Ⓒ Ⓓ	—— Ⓐ Ⓑ Ⓒ Ⓓ
—— Ⓕ Ⓖ Ⓗ Ⓙ	—— Ⓕ Ⓖ Ⓗ Ⓙ	—— Ⓕ Ⓖ Ⓗ Ⓙ
—— Ⓐ Ⓑ Ⓒ Ⓓ	—— Ⓐ Ⓑ Ⓒ Ⓓ	—— Ⓐ Ⓑ Ⓒ Ⓓ
—— Ⓐ Ⓑ Ⓒ Ⓓ	—— Ⓐ Ⓑ Ⓒ Ⓓ	—— Ⓐ Ⓑ Ⓒ Ⓓ
—— Ⓕ Ⓖ Ⓗ Ⓙ	—— Ⓕ Ⓖ Ⓗ Ⓙ	—— Ⓕ Ⓖ Ⓗ Ⓙ
—— Ⓐ Ⓑ Ⓒ Ⓓ	—— Ⓐ Ⓑ Ⓒ Ⓓ	—— Ⓐ Ⓑ Ⓒ Ⓓ
—— Ⓕ Ⓖ Ⓗ Ⓙ	—— Ⓕ Ⓖ Ⓗ Ⓙ	—— Ⓕ Ⓖ Ⓗ Ⓙ
—— Ⓐ Ⓑ Ⓒ Ⓓ	—— Ⓐ Ⓑ Ⓒ Ⓓ	—— Ⓐ Ⓑ Ⓒ Ⓓ
—— Ⓐ Ⓑ Ⓒ Ⓓ	—— Ⓐ Ⓑ Ⓒ Ⓓ	—— Ⓐ Ⓑ Ⓒ Ⓓ
—— Ⓕ Ⓖ Ⓗ Ⓙ	—— Ⓕ Ⓖ Ⓗ Ⓙ	—— Ⓕ Ⓖ Ⓗ Ⓙ
—— Ⓐ Ⓑ Ⓒ Ⓓ	—— Ⓐ Ⓑ Ⓒ Ⓓ	—— Ⓐ Ⓑ Ⓒ Ⓓ
—— Ⓕ Ⓖ Ⓗ Ⓙ	—— Ⓕ Ⓖ Ⓗ Ⓙ	—— Ⓕ Ⓖ Ⓗ Ⓙ
—— Ⓐ Ⓑ Ⓒ Ⓓ	—— Ⓐ Ⓑ Ⓒ Ⓓ	—— Ⓐ Ⓑ Ⓒ Ⓓ
—— Ⓐ Ⓑ Ⓒ Ⓓ	—— Ⓐ Ⓑ Ⓒ Ⓓ	—— Ⓐ Ⓑ Ⓒ Ⓓ
—— Ⓕ Ⓖ Ⓗ Ⓙ	—— Ⓕ Ⓖ Ⓗ Ⓙ	—— Ⓕ Ⓖ Ⓗ Ⓙ
—— Ⓐ Ⓑ Ⓒ Ⓓ	—— Ⓐ Ⓑ Ⓒ Ⓓ	—— Ⓐ Ⓑ Ⓒ Ⓓ
—— Ⓕ Ⓖ Ⓗ Ⓙ	—— Ⓕ Ⓖ Ⓗ Ⓙ	—— Ⓕ Ⓖ Ⓗ Ⓙ
—— Ⓐ Ⓑ Ⓒ Ⓓ	—— Ⓐ Ⓑ Ⓒ Ⓓ	—— Ⓐ Ⓑ Ⓒ Ⓓ
—— Ⓐ Ⓑ Ⓒ Ⓓ	—— Ⓐ Ⓑ Ⓒ Ⓓ	
—— Ⓕ Ⓖ Ⓗ Ⓙ	—— Ⓕ Ⓖ Ⓗ Ⓙ	
—— Ⓐ Ⓑ Ⓒ Ⓓ	—— Ⓐ Ⓑ Ⓒ Ⓓ	
—— Ⓕ Ⓖ Ⓗ Ⓙ	—— Ⓕ Ⓖ Ⓗ Ⓙ	
—— Ⓐ Ⓑ Ⓒ Ⓓ	—— Ⓐ Ⓑ Ⓒ Ⓓ	

Name _____ Date _____

MAP AND GLOBE SKILLS
Read a Map

Directions Use the map of the United States to answer these questions.

1 What does a star surrounded by a circle represent on the map? _national capital_

2 What two inset maps are part of this map? Why do you think those areas are shown in inset maps? _Alaska and Hawaii; because those two states are not physically connected to the continental United States_

3 What city is located in square B–3? _Boise, Idaho_

4 In which direction would you travel to go from Nebraska to Texas? _south_

5 About how many miles is it from Salem, Oregon, to Madison, Wisconsin?
about 1,500 miles

© Harcourt

Name _____   Date _____

Why Geography Matters

Directions Use the terms in the box below to complete the sentences.

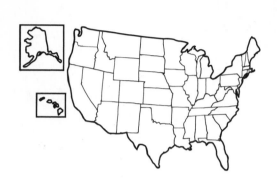

geography
geographers
location
physical features
human features
interact
region

1 Formed by nature, _____ physical features _____ include landforms, bodies of water, and plant life.

2 Because humans and their surroundings _____ interact _____, they affect one another.

3 When you study Earth and the people who live on it, you are studying _____ geography _____.

4 Buildings, roads, and cities are all examples of _____ human features _____.

5 A _____ region _____ is an area on Earth whose features make it different from other areas.

6 Every place on Earth has its own space, or _____ location _____.

7 _____ Geographers _____ do much more than find places on maps. They learn all they can about places and the people who live there.

Use after reading Introduction, Skill Lesson, pages 2–3.

Why History Matters

Directions Below are some homework assignments for a history class. Use the tasks listed in the box to identify the purpose of each assignment. Write the task in the space provided. You will use one of the tasks twice.

Learning About Time	**Identifying Points of View**
Finding Evidence	**Drawing Conclusions**

1 Read the letters in your textbook written by a woman who owned slaves during the Civil War. Then read the diary entries in your textbook written by one of her slaves who learned to read and write after she escaped to freedom. Use these two sources to understand the different ways people of that time period felt about their lives. Identifying Points of View _____

2 While you read Chapter 4 of your textbook, make a list of the major events that occurred before the American Revolution. Compare those events, and think about how they affected one another. Then analyze all the information together to decide why the American Revolution happened. Drawing Conclusions _____

3 Interview your grandparents or other family members about when your family first came to the United States. Ask to see old photographs, paintings, letters, birth certificates, or journals belonging to your family. Use all of these sources to write a report on the history of your family in the United States.

Finding Evidence _____

4 Do research at the library or on the Internet to find when the first settlers arrived in your state, when your state joined the United States, when your state capital was chosen, and other important events in your state's history. Then display the information in a time line titled "The History of My State."

Learning About Time _____

5 Do research at the library or on the Internet to find speeches given by the people who ran for President of the United States in the last election. Use these sources to understand the different opinions each person had on important issues at the time. Identifying Points of View _____

© Harcourt

READING SKILLS

Compare Primary and Secondary Sources

Directions Decide whether each of the items below is a primary or secondary source. Write *P* for a primary source or *S* for a secondary source in the space provided. Then under each item, explain your answer.

1 P _____ the United States Constitution

It is a document of its time.

2 S _____ a history textbook written today about an event that took place in 1861

It is not an eyewitness account.

3 S _____ a newspaper story written about a hurricane, based on the author's interviews of people who saw the storm

It is not an eyewitness account.

4 P _____ the transcript of a speech given by the President of the United States

It is a record of the President's exact words.

5 P _____ a soldier's diary describing a battle in which the soldier took part

It is an eyewitness account.

6 P _____ a photograph of a crime scene

It is an eyewitness account.

7 S _____ an encyclopedia article about the building of the pyramids

It is not an eyewitness account.

8 P _____ a videotape recording of a baseball game

It is an eyewitness account.

© Harcourt

Use after reading Introduction, Skill Lesson, pages 6–7.

Why Economics Matters

Directions Use the clues to complete the word puzzle. The shaded line of letters will show you the theme of the puzzle.

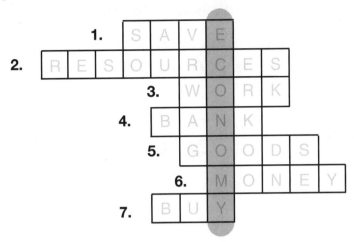

Clues

1 Most people ___*save*___ money to pay for college in the future.

2 An economy is the way people use ___*resources*___ to meet their needs.

3 Hospitals, schools, farms, and factories are just a few of the many places where people ___*work*___.

4 A ___*bank*___ is a place where people keep their money.

5 People make, buy, sell, and trade ___*goods*___ to meet their needs.

6 Most people have jobs or own businesses in order to make ___*money*___.

7 If you do not live and work on a farm, you probably ___*buy*___ most of the food you eat.

Why Civics and Government Matter

The United States government passes laws to help people live together peacefully and safely. Many of these laws describe the important rights and responsibilities you have as a citizen of the United States.

Directions Each right shown in the chart below is guaranteed by law in the United States. Complete the chart by describing why you think each right is important. Possible responses are given.

RIGHT	WHY IS IT IMPORTANT?
Freedom of speech	People should be allowed to say what they want and to express their opinions freely.
Freedom of religion	People should be free to worship the way they want.
Freedom to write and publish	People should be allowed to communicate information and their ideas to others.
The right to gather with other citizens	People should be allowed to discuss issues together or to belong to clubs or other organizations.
The right to ask the government for action or help in solving problems	The government works for the people, so people should be able to ask the government to do things.

© Harcourt

Use after reading Introduction, page 9.

Name ______________________ Date ____________

Why Culture and Society Matter

Directions Interview your family members to learn about your family's cultural heritage. Then complete the chart below. Responses will vary.

MY CULTURAL HERITAGE

My family name: ______________________

Where my early family members came from: ______________________

____

Languages my early family members spoke and languages my family speaks today: ______________________

____

Holidays my family celebrates: ______________________

____

____

Special ways of doing things that are part of my family's cultural heritage:

____

____

____

Special foods that are part of my family's cultural heritage:

____

____

____

Use after reading Introduction, page 10.

Where on Earth Is the United States?

Directions Complete the following activities to describe where the United States is on Earth. Possible responses are given.

1 In which hemispheres is the United States located?

The United States is located in the Northern and Western Hemispheres.

2 Which oceans and continents describe the global address of the United States?

The United States is located on the continent of North America, with the Pacific

Ocean to the west and the Atlantic Ocean to the east.

3 Describe the relative location of the United States, using its relation to other countries.

The United States is one of the three large countries that cover most of North

America. Canada forms the northern boundary of the United States, while

Mexico makes up the southwestern boundary.

4 Use bodies of water to describe the relative location of the United States.

The Pacific Ocean forms the western boundary, and the Atlantic Ocean forms

the eastern boundary of the United States. The Gulf of Mexico forms much of the

southern boundary of the United States.

5 Describe the location of your state in relation to other states in the United States.

Answers will vary depending on where

students live. Students should describe

their state's location in relation to other

states.

© Harcourt

MAP AND GLOBE SKILLS

Use Latitude and Longitude

The years between 1492 and 1522 are often called the Great Age of Exploration. During those years many European nations sent ships and explorers to look for new lands and riches. In fact, by the end of the Great Age of Exploration, Europeans had sailed all the way around the world!

Directions Use the map below to answer the questions on page 10.

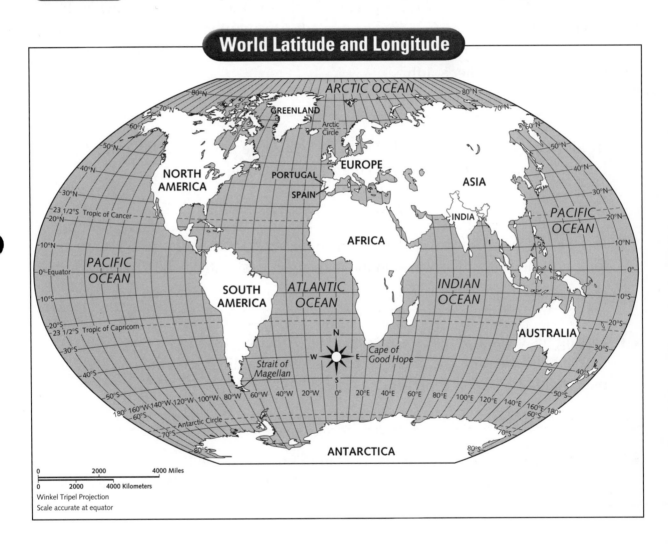

World Latitude and Longitude

(continued)

1 Between 1492 and 1522, most explorers set sail from two European countries that lie at latitude 40°N. Which countries are these?

Spain and Portugal

2 In 1488 Bartholomeu Dias sailed as far south as 35°S, 20°E before returning home to Europe. What continent did Dias reach?

Africa

3 Between 1492 and 1502, Christopher Columbus made four journeys across the Atlantic Ocean. On the first voyage, he sailed to about latitude 20°N. On his last voyage, Columbus reached a latitude of about 10°N. On which voyage did Columbus sail farther south?

last voyage (10°N)

4 In 1497 Giovanni Caboto landed near 50°N latitude in present-day Canada. Was he closer to the Arctic Circle or to the Antarctic Circle?

Arctic Circle

5 In 1498 Vasco da Gama sailed around the tip of Africa to India. Which lines of longitude and latitude shown on the map are closest to the southern tip of India?

10°N, 80°E

6 During his voyage between 1501 and 1502, Amerigo Vespucci crossed both the Tropic of Cancer and the Tropic of Capricorn. What line of latitude does each of these named parallels represent?

Tropic of Cancer = 23 1/2°N; Tropic of Capricorn = 23 1/2°S

7 Ferdinand Magellan was the first person to sail across the Pacific Ocean. Magellan began that part of his journey at about 55°S, 70°W. What place does this absolute location describe?

Strait of Magellan

© Harcourt

The Land

As early explorers, settlers, and visitors traveled throughout North America, they often described the land they saw. In many cases, their descriptions provided the first glimpses of the great variety of landforms in the United States.

Directions From the list of landforms in the United States below, choose one to match each of the descriptions that follow. In the space next to each quotation, write the name of the landform that the person described.

Appalachian Mountains	Grand Canyon
Central Valley	Great Basin
Coastal Plain	Great Plains
Columbia Plateau	Rocky Mountains

1 _Great_ _Basin_ — "A level, blasted region . . . Far as one could see . . . there was nothing but desert."
—British traveler Isabella Lucy Bird, 1873

2 _Coastal_ _Plain_ — "Our landing place . . . is mostly level; the soil is sand and earth. All throughout it there are very large trees."
—Spanish explorer Álvar Núñez Cabeza de Vaca, 1542

3 _Central_ _Valley_ — "Making your way through the mazes of the Coast Ranges . . . lies the great . . . valley glowing golden in the sunshine . . . one smooth, flowery, lake-like bed of fertile soil."
—American naturalist John Muir, 1868

4 _Appalachian_ _Mountains_ — "Mountains . . . running nearly parallel with the sea-coast . . . of the Atlantic."
—United States President Thomas Jefferson, 1781

5 _Great_ _Plains_ — "I reached some plains, so vast that I did not find their limit anywhere that I went . . . there was not a stone, nor a bit of rising ground, nor a tree, nor a shrub."
—Spanish explorer Francisco Vásquez de Coronado, 1541

6 _Rocky_ _Mountains_ — "Vast mountains of rock eternally covered with snow."
—American explorer William Clark, 1805

Name _____ Date _____

MAP AND GLOBE SKILLS
Read an Elevation Map

Directions Study this elevation map, and read each sentence below. Circle *T* if the sentence is true and *F* if it is false. If the sentence is false, cross out the word that makes it false and write above it the correct word to make it true.

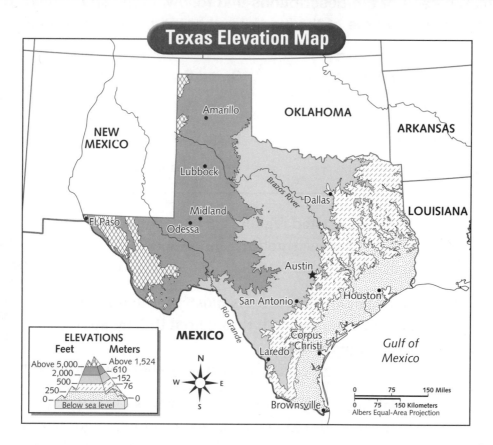

Texas Elevation Map

1. Lubbock has a higher elevation than Corpus Christi. Ⓣ F

2. The highest parts of Texas are located in the ~~south~~. *(west)* T Ⓕ

3. Most of Texas lies ~~below~~ sea level. *(above)* T Ⓕ

4. Brownsville has a lower elevation than Austin. Ⓣ F

5. ~~None~~ of the land along the Texas–New Mexico border is higher than 2,000 feet above sea level. *(All)* T Ⓕ

6. Austin and San Antonio are located in the same range of elevations. Ⓣ F

Use after reading Chapter 1, Skill Lesson, pages 34–35.

Name _____ Date _____

Looking at Rivers

Directions Use the map of Major Rivers of the United States on page 40 of your textbook to complete the following sentences.

1 The ____Yukon____ River flows across the entire state of Alaska.

2 The Mississippi River begins in the state of ____Minnesota____ and empties into the ____Gulf of Mexico____.

3 The ____Connecticut____ River forms most of the border between Vermont and New Hampshire.

4 The Platte River is a tributary of the ____Missouri____ River.

5 The Alabama River empties into the Gulf of Mexico near the city of ____Mobile, Alabama____.

6 A river called the ____Rio Grande____ forms much of the border between the United States and Mexico.

7 Five cities located along the Mississippi River are ____Minneapolis____, ____St. Louis____, ____Cairo____, ____Memphis____, and ____New Orleans____.

8 From Montana, the Missouri River flows east into the state of ____North Dakota____.

9 The city of Chicago is located on the ____Illinois____ River.

10 The Columbia River flows mostly through the state of ____Washington____.

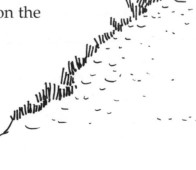

Use after reading Chapter 1, Lesson 3, pages 38–43.

Climate Across the United States

Because the United States is so large, it includes nearly every kind of climate known on Earth. In order to study and compare different climates, people often divide the world into climate regions. The areas within each region share similar average temperatures and precipitation levels.

Directions The chart on page 15 describes six main categories of climate on Earth. The map below it shows where these climate regions occur across the United States. Use the chart and map to answer the following questions.

1 What is the only state in the United States that has areas with a polar climate? Why do you think this kind of climate is found there? Alaska; because Alaska lies far north of the equator, it receives little heat from the sun.

2 Which states have areas with a tropical climate? How do those states' locations explain why they have this kind of climate? Hawaii and Florida; because those two states lie far south in the United States toward the equator; they are both surrounded by oceans, which brings greater humidity and higher precipitation levels.

3 What landform explains the parts of the United States that have a highland climate? mountains

4 In what landform region of the United States are most of the desert or semiarid climates located? the Intermountain Region

5 What are the main differences between a temperate warm climate and a temperate cold climate? How does location help explain these differences? Possible responses: Temperate cold climates have longer, colder winters and shorter summers than temperate warm climates. They lie either farther north of the equator or farther inland from the oceans.

(continued)

© Harcourt

REGION	CLIMATE
Tropical	Temperatures are usually very hot year-round. It can be rainy all year or have two seasons—one wet and one dry.
Desert or Semiarid	It is dry year-round or has only a short rainy season. Temperatures can be either hot or cold.
Temperate Warm	Rain falls throughout the year but is heaviest during the long summers. Summer temperatures are usually hot, and winters are short and mild.
Temperate Cold	Winters can be long, cold, and snowy. Summers are short but may be very hot.
Highland	High elevations bring cool or cold temperatures year-round.
Polar	Temperatures are very cold most of the year.

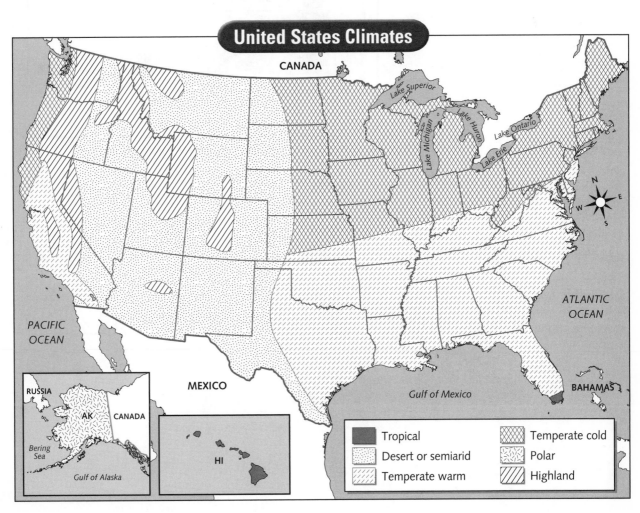

United States Climates

Natural Resources

Many of the products that people use every day are made from natural resources. Because natural resources are limited, conservation is very important. Waste from the products people use creates large amounts of garbage—about 230 million tons a year in the United States alone. By understanding this and limiting what we throw away, we can reduce the amount of garbage produced. This will help conserve resources and protect the environment.

Directions **Use the bar graph to answer these questions.**

1 What material makes up the largest part of the garbage produced in the United States each year?

paper

2 About how much glass do people in the United States throw away each year?

about 13 million tons

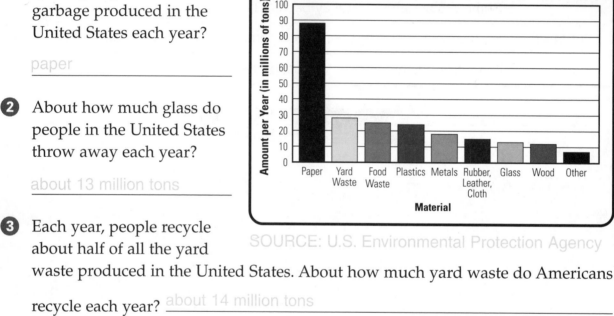

Garbage in the United States

SOURCE: U.S. Environmental Protection Agency

3 Each year, people recycle about half of all the yard waste produced in the United States. About how much yard waste do Americans recycle each year? about 14 million tons

4 What are some ways you and your family could cut down on the amount of garbage you throw away each day? Answers will vary but should include reusing and recycling materials. Other possible responses may include donating unwanted materials to charity; requesting not to receive junk mail; printing fewer computer files; and buying items in bulk rather than individually packaged.

© Harcourt

Name _____ Date _____

CHART AND GRAPH SKILLS
Use Tables to Group Information

In addition to preserving resources in national forests, the United States government also sets aside large areas of the country to preserve as national parks.

Directions Read the information in Table A about national parks in the United States. Classify that same information in Table B by size, from largest park to smallest park. Then use both tables to answer the questions that follow.

Table A: United States National Parks, in Alphabetical Order		
NATIONAL PARK	**LOCATION**	**ACRES**
Acadia	Maine	41,933
Badlands	South Dakota	242,756
Grand Canyon	Arizona	1,217,158
Great Smoky Mountains	North Carolina and Tennessee	520,269
Olympic	Washington	922,651
Yosemite	California	761,236

Table B: United States National Parks, in Order by Size		
ACRES	**LOCATION**	**NATIONAL PARK**
1,217,158	Arizona	Grand Canyon
922,651	Washington	Olympic
761,236	California	Yosemite
520,269	North Carolina and Tennessee	Great Smoky Mountains
242,756	South Dakota	Badlands
41,933	Maine	Acadia

SOURCE: U.S. National Parks Service

1 In which state is Olympic National Park located? In which table was it easier to find this information? Washington; Table A

2 Which park listed in the tables is the largest? In which table was it easier to find this information? Grand Canyon National Park; Table B

3 Where is Great Smoky Mountains National Park? Which table did you use to find this information? Explain why you used that table. North Carolina and Tennessee; Table A; because it is easier to find a park's name in an alphabetical list

4 In what other ways could you classify this information about national parks in tables? Possible responses: in alphabetical order by location; in order by size from smallest to largest

Our Country's Geography

Directions Use this graphic organizer to show that you understand how the chapter's main ideas are connected. Complete it by writing two details about each main idea.

There are many ways to describe locations in the United States.

1. Students should list ways to describe relative location— using hemispheres, nearby bodies of water,

2. or bordering countries—and absolute location— using lines of longitude and latitude.

People use natural resources.

1. Students should describe ways people use natural resources to meet their needs, such as plowing land to grow food, cutting trees for wood, using

2. minerals and fuels for energy and building, and using water to grow food and create energy.

The United States has many landforms.

1. Students should list major landforms described in Lesson 2,

2. such as mountains, plains, plateaus, valleys, and basins.

Our Country's Geography

Resources

Location

Landforms

Climate

Rivers

The climate varies across the United States for several reasons.

1. Students should list distance from the equator, location

2. on the continent, nearness to water or certain landforms, and elevation.

Rivers both wear down and build up the land.

1. Students should describe erosion and tell how rivers add soil

2. to floodplains and deltas.

Name _____   Date _____

Test Preparation

Directions Read each question and choose the best answer. Then fill in the circle for the answer you have chosen. Be sure to fill in the circle completely.

1 The United States is located on the continent of—
- Ⓐ Europe.
- Ⓑ South America.
- Ⓒ Asia.
- Ⓓ North America.

2 What mountains run along most of the Pacific Coast of the United States?
- Ⓕ Appalachian Mountains
- Ⓖ Rocky Mountains
- Ⓗ Sierra Nevada
- Ⓙ Coast Ranges

3 The place where a river empties into a larger body of water is called the river's—
- Ⓐ mouth.
- Ⓑ source.
- Ⓒ channel.
- Ⓓ floodplain.

4 Which of the following is *not* a factor that affects a place's weather?
- Ⓕ the precipitation
- Ⓖ the wind
- Ⓗ the economy
- Ⓙ the temperature

5 It is important to conserve fuels because those resources are—
- Ⓐ nonrenewable.
- Ⓑ expensive.
- Ⓒ renewable.
- Ⓓ polluted.

© Harcourt

Use after reading Chapter 1, pages 20–55.

Regions Around You

Directions Fill in the lines of the box below to describe where you live. Then in the diagram that follows, color your state on the map of the United States. In the state box, name your state. Then fill in the other boxes of the diagram to name the regions where you live.

WHERE I LIVE

NAME _Students should write their name._ _____

STREET ADDRESS _Students should write their address._ _____

CITY OR TOWN _Students should write their city or town._ _____

STATE _Students should write their state._ _____

REGION _Northeast, South, Middle West, or West_ _____

COUNTRY _United States_ _____

CONTINENT _North America_ _____

HEMISPHERES _Northern Hemisphere and Western Hemisphere_ _____

Check students' diagrams for correct state, county, and city labels.

Regions Within Regions

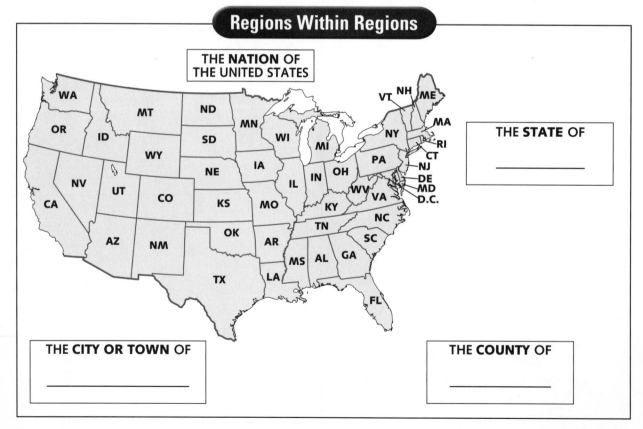

THE **NATION** OF THE UNITED STATES

THE **STATE** OF
_____

THE **CITY OR TOWN** OF
_____

THE **COUNTY** OF
_____

Use after reading Chapter 2, Lesson 1, pages 60–64.

Other Kinds of Regions

Directions Use the clues to fill in the words from 1 to 7. When you have finished, read the letters inside the shaded boxes from top to bottom to see the theme of this puzzle. A black box means a space between two words.

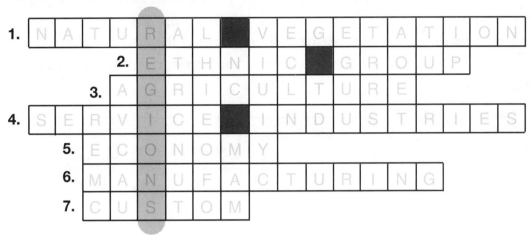

1. N A T U R A L ■ V E G E T A T I O N
2. E T H N I C ■ G R O U P
3. A G R I C U L T U R E
4. S E R V I C E ■ I N D U S T R I E S
5. E C O N O M Y
6. M A N U F A C T U R I N G
7. C U S T O M

Clues

1 the plant life that grows naturally in an area

2 a group made up of people from the same country, people of the same race, or people with a shared way of life

3 farming

4 industries in which workers are paid to do things for other people

5 the way the people of a region use resources to meet their needs

6 the making of products

7 a usual way of doing things

Name _____   Date _____

MAP AND GLOBE SKILLS
Use a Land Use and Resource Map

Directions Create a symbol for each resource or product listed in the table below. Then draw your symbol next to its label in the map key on page 23. Finally, use the completed table to draw the correct symbol on the map in the states listed for each resource or product. One resource, natural gas, has been completed as an example.

RESOURCE OR PRODUCT	SYMBOL	STATES
Oil		Texas, Alaska, California
Coal		Wyoming, West Virginia, Kentucky
Natural gas	🔥	Texas, Louisiana, Alaska
Chickens		Georgia, Arkansas, Alabama
Cattle		Texas, Nebraska, Kansas
Fish		Alaska, Louisiana, California
Lumber		Oregon, Washington, California
Cotton		Texas, California, Georgia
Wheat		Kansas, North Dakota, Montana
Corn		Iowa, Illinois, Nebraska
Citrus fruits		Florida, California, Texas

© Harcourt

(continued)

Name _____ Date _____

United States Land Use and Resources

CANADA

WA

MT

OR

ID

WY

SD

ND

MN

Lake Superior

WI

Lake Michigan

MI

Lake Huron

Lake Ontario

ME

VT

NH

MA

NY

Lake Erie

PA

RI

CT

NJ

DE

MD

NV

UT

CO

NE

IA

IL

IN

OH

WV

VA

KY

CA

AZ

NM

KS

MO

OK

AR

TN

NC

SC

ATLANTIC
OCEAN

PACIFIC
OCEAN

TX

LA

MS

AL

GA

N
W   E
S

FL

RUSSIA

AK

CANADA

Bering
Sea

Gulf of Alaska

0   250   500 Miles
0 250 500 Kilometers

MEXICO

HI

0   125   250 Miles
0 125 250 Kilometers

Gulf of Mexico

0   125   250 Miles
0   125   250 Kilometers
Albers Equal-Area Projection

	Manufacturing		Chickens
	Crops and livestock		Cattle
	Ranching or grazing		Fish
	Forest products		Lumber
	Little-used land		Cotton
	Oil		Wheat
	Coal		Corn
⬣	Natural gas		Citrus fruits

Name _____ Date _____

Regions Change and Connect

Directions Advances in technology often cause regions to change and connect. The table below lists some important events in the history of transportation and communication in the United States. Complete the time line below by writing the letter of each event from the table at its correct date on the time line.

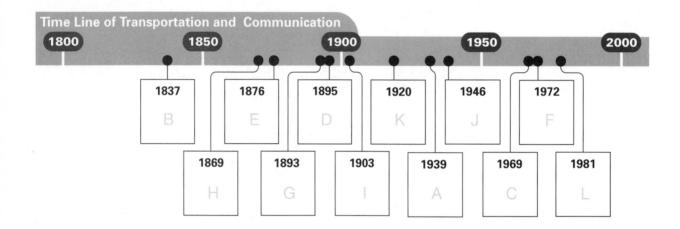

A	In 1939 television broadcasting begins in the United States.
B	The telegraph, which sends messages over wires, is invented in 1837.
C	In 1969 American astronauts become the first people to walk on the moon.
D	Wireless telegraph is invented in 1895.
E	In 1876 the telephone is invented.
F	Electronic mail, or e-mail, is introduced for the Internet in 1972.
G	In 1893 the first gasoline-powered automobile is built in the United States.
H	Coast-to-coast railroad service across the United States begins in 1869.
I	In 1903 Americans conduct the first successful airplane flight.
J	Americans build the first fully electronic digital computer in 1946.
K	Radio broadcasting begins in the United States in 1920.
L	In 1981 the first space shuttle is launched from the United States.

© Harcourt

Use after reading Chapter 2, Lesson 3, pages 72–77.

Name _____ Date _____

Identify Cause and Effect

Regions of the United States are constantly changing for a variety of reasons. Events and changes that happen in a region sometimes cause other events and changes to take place. Below are some of those events and changes. What caused them? What effects have those causes produced?

Directions Use your textbook's information about different regions in the United States to complete the following cause-and-effect chart.

CAUSE	→	EFFECT
Wind and water wore down the peaks of the Appalachian Mountains over time.	→	The peaks of the Appalachians are now rounded and much lower than those of the Rocky Mountains.
Rivers flooded and water spread out over floodplains and deltas. The floodwaters left behind silt.	→	**Silt built up along floodplains and deltas and made the land there very fertile.**
People built dams on several rivers in the Phoenix, Arizona, area.	→	More fresh water and electricity allowed more people to live and work there.
Several theme parks opened in and near Orlando, Florida.	→	**Tourism became the largest industry in the Orlando, Florida, area.**
Cars, trains, airplanes, telephones, computers, and televisions were invented.	→	Travel and communication became faster and easier.

© Harcourt

Regions Around the World

Directions The facts below describe different kinds of regions around the world. Use pages 79–83 in your textbook to classify the information according to the kind of region that each fact describes. In the blank next to each fact, write *PA* for a physical region of Asia, *CA* for a cultural region of Africa, or *PE* for a political region of Europe.

1 __PA__ The ten tallest mountains in the world are part of the Himalayas.

2 __CA__ The Ashanti (uh•SHAN•tee) people of Ghana wear clothes decorated with repeating patterns. The patterns have meanings, which the Ashanti "read" like poems.

3 __PE__ Vatican City and Monaco are the two smallest countries in the world.

4 __CA__ During the month-long religious holiday of Ramadan (RAH•muh•dahn), Islamic people fast, or do not eat, during the daytime.

5 __PE__ The country of Switzerland is divided into 26 regions, called *cantons*, which are similar to our states.

6 __PA__ So many needleleaf trees cover southern Siberia that people often call the region a "green ocean."

7 __CA__ The Lingala language of the Congo River area has only one word to mean both "yesterday" and "today." The meaning depends on how people use the word.

8 __PA__ About four-fifths of the island nation of Indonesia is covered by rain forests.

9 __PE__ Rome, the capital of Italy, was the first city in the world to have more than 1 million residents.

10 __PA__ If there were a flight of stairs rising from the bottom of the Dead Sea, you would have to climb about 2,000 steps to reach sea level!

Name _____ Date _____

Looking at Regions

Directions Use this graphic organizer to summarize the main topics of this chapter. For each main topic, write some important details related to the topic. Then write a brief statement to summarize the main idea of the topic.

Possible responses are given.

Looking at Regions

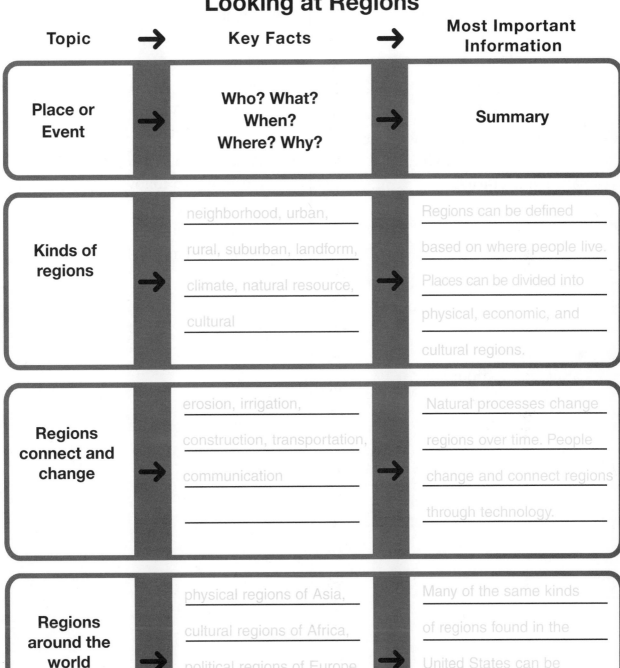

Topic →	Key Facts →	Most Important Information
Place or Event	Who? What? When? Where? Why?	Summary
Kinds of regions	neighborhood, urban, rural, suburban, landform, climate, natural resource, cultural	Regions can be defined based on where people live. Places can be divided into physical, economic, and cultural regions.
Regions connect and change	erosion, irrigation, construction, transportation, communication	Natural processes change regions over time. People change and connect regions through technology.
Regions around the world	physical regions of Asia, cultural regions of Africa, political regions of Europe	Many of the same kinds of regions found in the United States can be found in places around the world.

© Harcourt

Use after reading Chapter 2, pages 58–83.

Name _____   Date _____

Test Preparation

Directions Read each question, and choose the best answer. Then fill in the circle for the answer you have chosen. Be sure to fill in the circle completely.

1 Most Americans live in—
- Ⓐ rural regions.
- Ⓑ mountain regions.
- Ⓒ urban regions.
- Ⓓ suburban regions.

2 In what kind of industry do factory workers earn their living?
- Ⓕ manufacturing
- Ⓖ mining
- Ⓗ agriculture
- Ⓙ service

3 Shaking hands when you meet someone is an example of—
- Ⓐ an industry.
- Ⓑ a custom.
- Ⓒ an ethnic group.
- Ⓓ technology.

4 Which of the following is *not* a form of communication?
- Ⓕ telephones
- Ⓖ railroads
- Ⓗ fax machines
- Ⓙ computers

5 What religion do most people in North Africa follow?
- Ⓐ Judaism
- Ⓑ Christianity
- Ⓒ Buddhism
- Ⓓ Islam

© Harcourt

Use after reading Chapter 2, pages 58–83.

New England Through the Years

When the Pilgrims left England, they had planned to settle much farther south along the Atlantic Coast of North America, in what is now Virginia. But the *Mayflower* was blown off course by storms and reached the coast of present-day Massachusetts instead. The Pilgrims decided to make the best of the situation and start their colony there. The first thing they did—even before unloading the ship—was to write and sign the Mayflower Compact to agree on the laws they would all follow.

Directions **Read the contents of the Mayflower Compact below. Then use a dictionary to figure out the meaning of each word in bold print. Match each word to its correct meaning on page 30. Write the word in the blank beside the meaning that fits best. Then answer the questions that follow.**

The Mayflower Compact

In the name of God, Amen. We, whose names are underwritten, the Loyal Subjects of our dread Sovereign Lord, King James, by the Grace of God, of Great Britain, France and Ireland, King, Defender of the Faith, etc.

Having undertaken for the Glory of God, and Advancement of the Christian Faith, and the Honour of our King and Country, a voyage to plant the first colony in the northern Parts of Virginia; do by these Presents, solemnly and **mutually** in the Presence of God and one of another, **covenant** and combine ourselves together into a **civil** Body Politick, for our better Ordering and Preservation, and Furtherance of the Ends aforesaid;

And by Virtue hereof to **enact**, constitute, and frame, such just and equal Laws, **Ordinances**, Acts, **Constitutions** and Offices, from time to time, as shall be thought most meet and convenient for the General Good of the Colony; unto which we promise all due **Submission** and Obedience.

In Witness whereof we have hereunto **subscribed** our names at Cape Cod the eleventh of November, in the Reign of our Sovereign Lord, King James of England, France and Ireland the eighteenth, and of Scotland the fifty-fourth.

Anno Domini, 1620.

© Harcourt

(continued)

Name _____ Date _____

1 ____enact____ to make into a law **5** ____ordinance____ a law or set of laws

2 ____mutually____ together, jointly, in common **6** ____civil____ of a community of citizens or their government

3 ____constitution____ a plan showing the way in which a government, state, or society is organized **7** ____submission____ the act of giving in to the power of another or others

4 ____covenant____ a serious agreement or contract **8** ____subscribed____ signed one's name at the end of a document to show consent

9 Where were the Pilgrims when they wrote the Mayflower Compact?

Cape Cod, in present-day Massachusetts, on the *Mayflower*

10 On what date did the Pilgrims write that they signed the Mayflower Compact?

November 11, 1620

11 Who was the king of England and Ireland when the compact was written?

King James

12 In what part of North America did the Pilgrims write that they would "plant the first colony"? in the northern parts of Virginia

13 What three reasons did the Pilgrims list for voyaging to North America and starting a colony there? for the glory of God; for the advancement of the Christian faith; for the honor of their king and country

14 What do you think the Pilgrims meant when they said the purpose of the Mayflower Compact was "for our better Ordering and Preservation" and "for the General Good of the Colony"? Answers will vary but students should show an understanding that the purpose of laws and governments is to create an organized society that protects the lives and rights of its citizens.

Use after reading Chapter 3, Lesson 1, pages 100–105.

© Harcourt

CHART AND GRAPH SKILLS
Read a Time Line

Many time lines run horizontally from left to right across a page. Other time lines are vertical. A vertical time line lists events in order from top to bottom. The earliest date appears at the top of the time line. The latest date is listed at the bottom of the time line.

Directions Use the time line to answer the following questions.

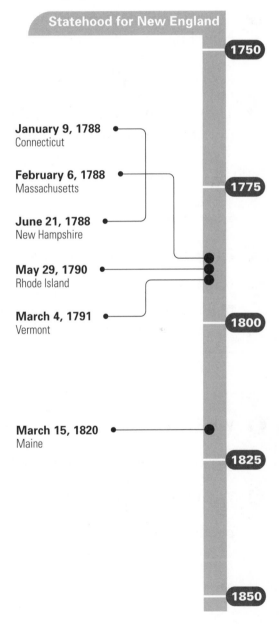

1 How many years does this time line cover?

100 years or one century

2 Into what equal time periods is this time line divided?

25 years

3 Which New England state joined the United States first?

Connecticut

4 What was the last New England state to join the United States?

Maine

5 In what year did three parts of New England become states?

1788

6 Could you label the founding of Plymouth Colony on this time line? Why or why not?

No, because the Pilgrims founded

Plymouth Colony in 1620 and that date is

not shown on this time line.

The New England Countryside

Directions Use the map of New England to answer these questions.

1 What two bodies of water form the southern and eastern boundaries of New England? the Atlantic Ocean and Long Island Sound

2 Where are the lowest elevations in New England?

along the Coastal Plain

3 Through which New England states does the Connecticut River flow?

It forms part of the border between

Vermont and New Hampshire, and then flows through Massachusetts and Connecticut.

4 What mountains make up the highest elevations in New England?

the Green and White Mountains

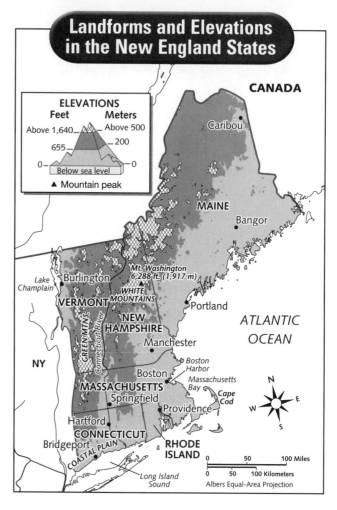

5 Which New England state borders Lake Champlain? What is the elevation of most of the land around this lake? Vermont; 0–655 feet (0–200 meters)

6 What is the elevation of Mount Washington? In which New England state is this peak located? 6,288 feet (1,917 m); New Hampshire

A New England Town

Directions Complete this table to compare Newfane, Vermont, in the past to Newfane, Vermont, today.

TOPIC	NEWFANE, 1800s	NEWFANE, 2000s
Arrangement of buildings	They were built around or on the town common.	They are built around or on the town common.
Uses of the town common	as a pasture for farm animals	as a public park for picnics, concerts, and festivals
The economy	Most people were farmers or worked in textile or lumber mills.	Most people work in service industries, especially tourism.
Transportation and communication	horses and wagons, railroads, letters	cars, airplanes, electricity, computers, telephones, televisions
Local government	People attended town meetings to make decisions about the town.	People attend town meetings to make decisions about the town.

© Harcourt

CITIZENSHIP SKILLS
Solve a Problem

Directions At a recent town meeting, the citizens of Newfane, Vermont, decided how to solve the problem of caring for stray dogs and cats found in their area. Use the graphic organizer below to think of ways to solve the same problem in your community. Look for understanding of problem-solving steps in students' responses.

IDENTIFY THE PROBLEM.

⬇

THINK OF POSSIBLE SOLUTIONS.

⬇

COMPARE SOLUTIONS AND SELECT THE BEST ONE.

⬇

PLAN HOW TO CARRY OUT THE SOLUTION.

⬇

SOLVE THE PROBLEM AND EVALUATE THE SOLUTION.

© Harcourt

Towns and Villages Around the World

Like many towns in the United States, towns and villages around the world often have town seals that are used on official documents. People in those towns usually design the seals to celebrate the town's history, the people who live there, a special building in town, or an unusual physical feature, industry, or attraction.

Directions Use the lines to the left of each blank circle below to list some features of the town or village that is named. Then use your lists to design town seals for these places in the blank circles.

HAWKSHEAD, ENGLAND

_____

_____

_____

_____

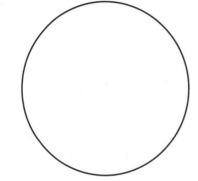

TENTERFIELD, AUSTRALIA

_____

_____

_____

_____

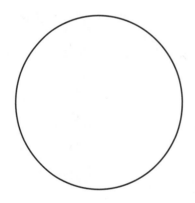

ST. ANDREWS, CANADA

_____

_____

_____

_____

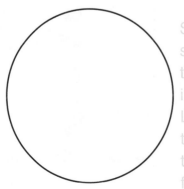

Students should use the information in Chapter 3, Lesson 4, of their textbooks to create lists of features for the three towns. Then they should use their lists to design a town seal for each place. Look for creative expression of geography themes in students' town seal designs.

© Harcourt

Use after reading Chapter 3, Lesson 4, pages 118–121.

Name _____ Date _____

New England States

Directions Use this graphic organizer to make generalizations about some of the main ideas in the chapter. Read each set of facts about New England. Then make a generalization based on those facts.

New England States

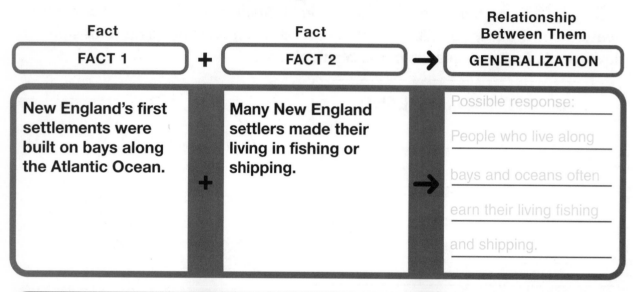

Fact	Fact	Relationship Between Them
FACT 1 +	**FACT 2** →	**GENERALIZATION**
New England's first settlements were built on bays along the Atlantic Ocean. +	**Many New England settlers made their living in fishing or shipping.** →	Possible response: People who live along bays and oceans often earn their living fishing and shipping.
Much of coastal New England has rocky soil, and it is difficult to grow many crops there. +	**Much of the New England countryside has rocky soil, and it is difficult to grow many crops there.** →	Possible response: Where the soil is rocky, it is difficult to grow many crops.
Many small towns in New England hold town meetings. +	**Town meetings allow residents to participate in their local government.** →	Possible response: Many residents of small towns in New England participate in their local government.

Use after reading Chapter 3, pages 98–121.

Name _____ Date _____

3 Test Preparation

Directions Read each question and choose the best answer. Then fill in the circle for the answer you have chosen. Be sure to fill in the circle completely.

1 The first European settlement in New England was built along—
Ⓐ Massachusetts Bay.
Ⓑ the Blackstone River.
Ⓒ the Connecticut River.
Ⓓ Plymouth Bay.

2 Which of the following is *not* a major crop grown in New England?
Ⓕ apples
Ⓖ potatoes
Ⓗ cotton
Ⓙ cranberries

3 Stone is mined in a—
Ⓐ factory.
Ⓑ quarry.
Ⓒ glacier.
Ⓓ common.

4 In what way do people in many New England towns participate in local government?
Ⓕ by attending town meetings
Ⓖ by volunteering at fund-raisers
Ⓗ by working in the tourist industry
Ⓙ by preserving historical sites

5 Why do people in the United States, Australia, and parts of Canada speak English?
Ⓐ because each of those places was once a British colony
Ⓑ because most people in each of those places have English ancestors
Ⓒ because all of those places border the country of England
Ⓓ because all of those places are part of the United Kingdom

Use after reading Chapter 3, pages 98–121.

The Middle Atlantic Colonies

By 1775, the year before the American colonists declared their independence from Britain, more than 2 million people lived in the 13 colonies along the Atlantic Coast. Who were the colonists, and where did they come from?

Directions Use the information in the pictograph below to answer the questions that follow.

Ethnic Groups in the 13 Colonies, 1775

ETHNIC GROUP	ESTIMATED POPULATION
English	👤👤 🧍🧍🧍🧍🧍🧍🧍🧍🧍🧍🧍🧍🧍🧍🧍🧍🧍🧍🧍🧍🧍🧍🧍🧍
African	👤
Swedish	🧍 ι
French	🧍🧍🧍 ι
Dutch	🧍🧍🧍🧍🧍🧍🧍
Scottish	🧍🧍🧍🧍🧍🧍🧍🧍🧍🧍🧍🧍🧍🧍🧍 ι
German	🧍🧍🧍🧍🧍🧍🧍🧍🧍🧍🧍🧍🧍🧍🧍🧍🧍 ι
Scotch-Irish	🧍🧍🧍🧍🧍🧍🧍🧍🧍🧍🧍🧍🧍🧍🧍🧍🧍 ι
Other	🧍🧍🧍🧍🧍🧍🧍🧍🧍🧍🧍🧍 ι

👤 = 500,000 people   🧍 = 10,000 people

1 From what country did almost half of all the colonists come? _England_

2 What was the second-largest ethnic group in the colonies in 1775? _African people_

3 Were there more French colonists or Swedish colonists? _French colonists_

4 About how many people from Germany lived in the colonies? _about 170,000 people_

5 What does the category "Other" mean in this pictograph?

It represents the people living in the colonies in 1775 who did not belong to any

of the ethnic groups listed on the pictograph.

© Harcourt

READING SKILLS
Identify Fact and Opinion

Directions American colonists made each of the statements below about declaring their independence from Britain. Read each statement, and decide whether it states a fact or an opinion. Write *F* beside a statement of fact, and write *O* beside a statement of opinion.

1 __F__ "Yesterday . . . a resolution was passed, without one dissenting colony, that these United Colonies are, and of right ought to be, free and independent States."
—John Adams, Letter to Abigail Adams,
  Philadelphia, July 3, 1776

2 __O__ "These are the times that try men's souls. . . . the harder the conflict, the more glorious the triumph."
—Thomas Paine, *The American Crisis*, December 23, 1776

3 __O__ "I know not what course others may take, but as for me, give me liberty or give me death!"
—Patrick Henry, Speech given at the Virginia
  Convention, March 23, 1775

4 __F__ "It has been determined by Congress, that the whole army raised for the defense of the American cause shall be put under my . . . command."
—George Washington, Letter to Martha
  Washington, Philadelphia, June 18, 1775

5 __O__ "We must all hang together, or assuredly we shall all hang separately."
—Benjamin Franklin, Philadelphia, July 4, 1776

6 __O__ ". . . whenever any form of government becomes destructive . . . it is the right of the people to alter or to abolish [end] it."
—Thomas Jefferson, *Declaration
  of Independence*, July 4, 1776

© Harcourt

Transportation and Growth

Directions Use the map of the Middle Atlantic states to answer these questions.

1 Where is the largest area of manufacturing in the Middle Atlantic region?

in the area around New York City

and Newark, New Jersey

2 What fuel resources are found in the Middle Atlantic states?

coal and oil or natural gas

3 How is most of the land in Delaware used?

for general farming

4 Where in the Middle Atlantic region are large areas of land used for growing fruits and vegetables?

along the Great Lakes and in the southern part of central Pennsylvania

5 Which Middle Atlantic state has the least forest land?

Delaware

6 How does this map help explain why a large steel industry developed in western Pennsylvania?

The map shows that both iron and coal are found in western Pennsylvania,

and both of those resources are needed to produce steel.

Land Use and Resources in the Middle Atlantic States

CANADA

VT   NH

Lake Ontario   NY

Utica   Albany

Rochester   Syracuse   MA

Lake Erie   Buffalo   Binghampton   CT

Erie   Scranton

PA   Newark

Allentown   New York

Pittsburgh   Harrisburg   NJ

Philadelphia   Trenton

Baltimore   N

MD   Dover

Washington, D.C.   DE

WV

VA   ATLANTIC OCEAN

▨ Manufacturing		☒	Coal
▨ General farming		☐	Iron
☐ Dairy farming		◈	Zinc
☐ Forest		⚒	Oil or natural gas
☐ Fruits and vegetables			

Use after reading Chapter 4, Lesson 2, pages 134–139.

© Harcourt

MAP AND GLOBE SKILLS

Use a Road Map and Mileage Table

Directions Use the mileage table below and the road map on page 42 to answer these questions.

1 Which interstate highway links Minnesota and Texas? Interstate 35

2 Which highway would take you from Los Angeles, California, to Portland, Oregon? What is the mileage between those two places? Interstate 5; 959 miles

3 List three cities through which Interstate Highway 80 passes. Responses may include San Francisco, Salt Lake City, Omaha, Des Moines, Chicago, Cleveland, and New York City.

4 Which east-west interstate highway runs the farthest south? Interstate 10

5 If you want to drive from Denver, Colorado, to Kansas City, Missouri, which highway could you take? How many miles would you have to drive?

Interstate 70; 600 miles

6 Which highway should you take if you want to start on the Pacific Coast, cross the Rocky Mountains, cross the Mississippi River, travel near the Great Lakes, and end up on the Atlantic Coast? Interstate 90 or 80

7 What is the mileage between New York City and Miami, Florida? What highway connects those two cities? 1,284 miles; Interstate 95

United States Road Mileage						
	Denver, CO	Kansas City, MO	Los Angeles, CA	Miami, FL	New York City, NY	Portland, OR
Denver, CO		600	1,059	2,066	1,771	1,238
Kansas City, MO	600		1,589	1,464	1,198	1,809
Los Angeles, CA	1,059	1,589		2,735	2,786	959
Miami, FL	2,066	1,464	2,735		1,284	3,260
New York City, NY	1,771	1,198	2,786	1,284		2,855
Portland, OR	1,238	1,809	959	3,260	2,855	

(continued)

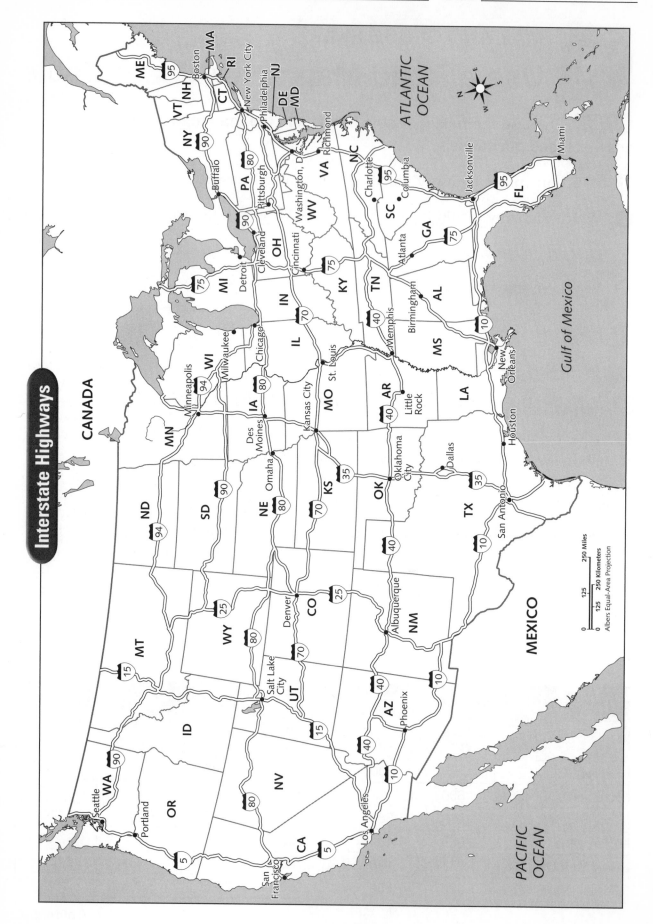

Interstate Highways

Use after reading Chapter 4, Skill Lesson, pages 140–141.

Cities Grow and Change

Directions The following excerpt is from the book *Immigrant Kids* by Russell Freedman. It describes what typical public schools in New York City were like during the early 1900s. Read the excerpt. Then, on the lines below, write a paragraph comparing and contrasting early city schools with your school today.

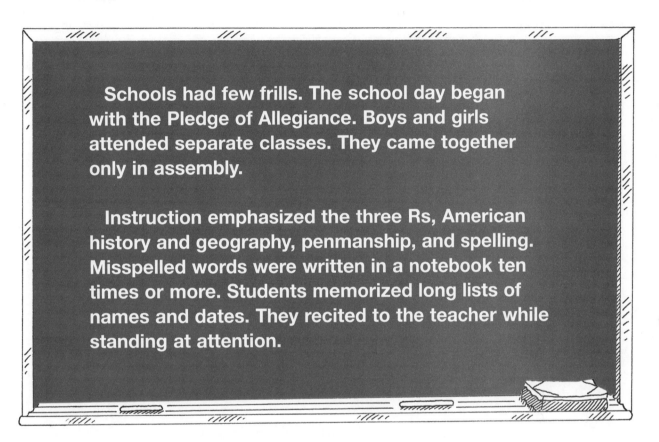

Schools had few frills. The school day began with the Pledge of Allegiance. Boys and girls attended separate classes. They came together only in assembly.

Instruction emphasized the three Rs, American history and geography, penmanship, and spelling. Misspelled words were written in a notebook ten times or more. Students memorized long lists of names and dates. They recited to the teacher while standing at attention.

Students should compare and contrast details described in the excerpt with details about their own class and school. Possible similarities: Some schools today still start the day with the Pledge of Allegiance; the same subjects are still studied today; notebooks are still used today. Possible differences: Boys and girls usually attend classes together today; students today study a greater variety of subjects; schools today use textbooks and computers.

Cities Around the World

Directions Use the maps in your textbook to complete this table. Then use the information in the table to answer the questions that follow.

Largest Urban Areas in the World, 2000			
Urban Area	**Country**	**Continent**	**Population**
Mumbai (Bombay)	India	Asia	18,066,000
Buenos Aires	Argentina	South America	12,560,000
Kolkata (Calcutta)	India	Asia	12,918,000
Lagos	Nigeria	Africa	13,427,000
Los Angeles	United States	North America	13,140,000
Mexico City	Mexico	North America	18,131,000
New York City	United States	North America	16,640,000
São Paulo	Brazil	South America	17,755,000
Shanghai	China	Asia	12,887,000
Tokyo	Japan	Asia	26,444,000

SOURCE: *World Almanac*, 2001

1 What urban area has the largest population in the world?

Tokyo, Japan

2 What are the two largest urban areas in the United States?

New York City and Los Angeles

3 What is the largest urban area in Africa? How many people live there?

Lagos, Nigeria; 13,427,000 people

4 How many people live in Mexico City?

18,131,000 people

5 How many of the ten largest urban areas in the world are located in Asia?

four

© Harcourt

Middle Atlantic States

Directions Complete this graphic organizer to show that you understand the causes and effects of some of the key events in the history of the Middle Atlantic states. Possible responses are given.

MIDDLE ATLANTIC STATES

CAUSE → **EFFECT**

| Many early settlements in the Middle Atlantic region were built along rivers or near the Atlantic Ocean. | Many settlements grew into large, busy port cities. |

| The British government passed new laws that forced the American colonists to pay taxes. | The American colonists became angry about taxation without representation and declared their independence from Britain. |

| Roads, canals, and railroads were built across the Appalachian Mountains. | More people and businesses moved to the western part of the Middle Atlantic region. |

| New industries developed in the region, and millions of people moved to the cities for jobs. | Cities in the Middle Atlantic region grew rapidly. |

Name _____ Date _____

4 Test Preparation

Directions Read each question, and choose the best answer. Then fill in the circle for the answer you have chosen. Be sure to fill in the circle completely.

1 Why did many port cities grow up in the Middle Atlantic region?

Ⓐ because they were built near the Appalachian Mountains

Ⓑ because shipbuilding was the largest industry in the region

Ⓒ because they were built along major rivers near the Atlantic Coast

Ⓓ because the region was the center for the nation's steel industry

2 Who wrote most of the Declaration of Independence?

Ⓕ Benjamin Franklin

Ⓖ Thomas Jefferson

Ⓗ George Washington

Ⓙ Thomas Paine

3 People built the Erie Canal to link—

Ⓐ Lake Erie and the Hudson River.

Ⓑ Lake Erie and Lake Ontario.

Ⓒ New York City and Philadelphia.

Ⓓ the St. Lawrence River and the Atlantic Ocean.

4 Why did many people move to Middle Atlantic cities in the late 1800s and early 1900s?

Ⓕ to attend colleges and universities

Ⓖ to buy their own land

Ⓗ for low-cost housing

Ⓙ for factory jobs

5 Which of the following is *not* a solution for problems in many urban areas around the world?

Ⓐ recycling programs

Ⓑ public transportation

Ⓒ unemployment

Ⓓ laws to limit pollution

© Harcourt

Use after reading Chapter 4, pages 124–155.

Settling the Region

Directions Many early settlers along the Fall Line built waterwheels on rivers to run mills that ground wheat into flour. Use this illustration to help you follow the process of using waterpower to produce flour. In each blank, write a number from 1 to 6 to order the steps.

A. ___5___ The turning of the mill post makes the grinding stone spin.

B. ___2___ The river water flows over the waterwheel.

C. ___1___ A stone dam built across the river forces the river water to pour through a small opening.

D. ___6___ The turning stone grinds the wheat into flour.

E. ___3___ The force of the rushing river water causes the waterwheel to turn.

F. ___4___ The turning of the waterwheel causes a post inside the mill to turn.

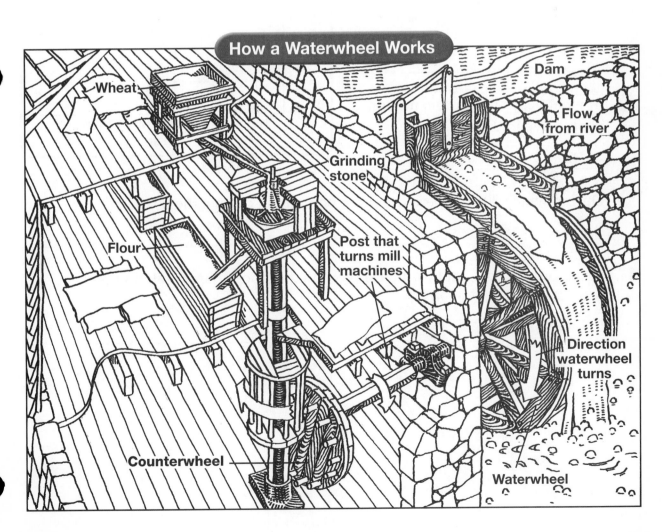

How a Waterwheel Works

Wheat

Dam

Flow from river

Grinding stone

Flour

Post that turns mill machines

Direction waterwheel turns

Counterwheel

Waterwheel

© Harcourt

Name _____ Date _____

CHART AND GRAPH SKILLS
Read a Line Graph

Directions After pioneers cleared the Wilderness Road, thousands of settlers crossed the Appalachian Mountains. As a result, the populations of what are now the Appalachian states of Kentucky, Tennessee, and West Virginia changed rapidly. Use the line graph below to answer the following questions about how the population of those states changed over time.

1 How has the population of the Appalachian states changed in the past 210 years?

It has increased.

2 About how many people lived in the Appalachian states in 1850?

about 2 million people (actual

population was 2,287,435)

3 In what year did nearly 6 million people live in those states?

1910

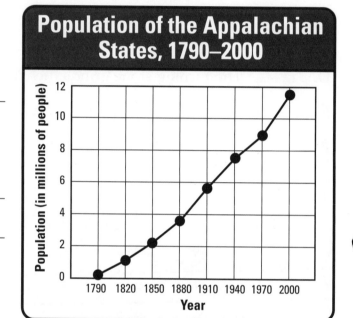

Population of the Appalachian States, 1790–2000

SOURCE: U.S. Census Bureau

4 During which 30-year period did the population change the most?

between 1970 and 2000

5 Based on this line graph, what can you predict about the population of the Appalachian states in 2030?

It will be greater than 12 million.

Use after reading Chapter 5, Skill Lesson, pages 178–179.

© Harcourt

People Use Natural Resources

Directions Complete this graphic organizer to show how natural resources in the Atlantic Coast and Appalachian states are connected to some of the region's industries and products.

NATURAL RESOURCE ➡	INDUSTRY ➡	PRODUCT
Fertile soil ➡	Agriculture ➡	Peanuts, soybeans, and cotton
Chesapeake Bay ➡	Fishing ➡	Fish and shellfish
Forests ➡	Manufacturing ➡	Furniture
Minerals and fuels ➡	Mining ➡	Coal
Grassy pastures ➡	Agriculture ➡	Horses
Hydroelectric power ➡	Manufacturing ➡	Aluminum
Clay, trees, plants, and sheep's wool ➡	Arts and crafts ➡	Baskets, blankets, pottery, and carvings
Cotton crops ➡	Manufacturing ➡	Denim and other kinds of cloth

Cities Grow and Industries Change

Like cities everywhere, cities in the Atlantic Coast and Appalachian region have grown for many different reasons. Some grew because of shipping and trade or new industries. Others grew because they were centers of state and national governments. Still others grew because of the many tourist attractions they offer.

Directions Use pages 186–191 of your textbook to find the names of cities that have grown in the Atlantic Coast and Appalachian region. Then write the names of those cities under the correct headings in the chart below. Some cities may be listed under more than one category.

Atlantic Coast and Appalachian Cities			
CENTERS OF SHIPPING AND TRADE	**CENTERS OF NEW INDUSTRIES**	**CENTERS OF GOVERNMENT**	**CENTERS OF TOURISM**
Possible listings:	Possible listings:	Possible listings:	Possible listings:
Baltimore, Maryland;	Nashville,	Richmond,	Jamestown,
Hampton, Newport	Tennessee;	Arlington, and	Williamsburg,
News, Norfolk, and	Lexington and	Norfolk, Virginia;	Yorktown, and
Richmond, Virginia;	Louisville,	Raleigh, North	Virginia Beach,
Charlotte and	Kentucky; Chapel	Carolina;	Virginia;
Raleigh, North	Hill, Durham, and	Annapolis and	Washington, D.C.;
Carolina; Memphis,	Raleigh, North	Baltimore,	Nashville,
Knoxville, and	Carolina	Maryland;	Tennessee;
Chattanooga,		Washington, D.C.;	Louisville,
Tennessee;		Charleston, West	Kentucky;
Louisville and		Virginia	Charlotte, North
Paducah, Kentucky			Carolina

© Harcourt

National Parks Around the World

Directions Read the descriptions of the national parks below. Then, in the blank next to each park's name, identify what that park preserves or protects. Write *WL* for wildlife, *NR* for natural resources, or *CH* for culture or history.

1 __WL__ **Galápagos National Park, South America** In 1959 Ecuador set aside nearly all of the islands along its Pacific Coast as a national park. Penguins and sea lions live in the park with iguanas and other tropical wildlife. The park's giant tortoises have one of the longest lifespans on Earth—up to 150 years!

2 __WL__ **Komodo National Park, Asia** The main purpose of this national park in Indonesia is to protect the oldest, largest, and one of the rarest reptiles in the world—the Komodo Dragon. This gigantic reptile lives nowhere else on Earth.

3 __CH__ **Kakadu National Park, Australia** Scientists in this national park have found evidence of the earliest human settlement in Australia. Some cave paintings there are nearly 20,000 years old! Many sites in the park are of great religious importance to the Aborigines, or the native people of Australia.

4 __NR__ **Skaftafell National Park, Europe** Founded in 1956, this national park in Iceland preserves an area called the Glacier Country. Visitors to the park can see huge icebergs, ice-blue glacial lakes, shimmering ice tunnels, frozen waterfalls, and miles of thick birch forests.

5 __WL__ **Garamba National Park, Africa** This park in the Democratic Republic of the Congo protects one of the most endangered animals in the world—the white rhinoceros. Only about 30 of these large animals still survive in the wild. People used to hunt them for their horns, but this is not allowed anymore. In fact, armed guards now protect the white rhinoceroses at the park.

© Harcourt

Atlantic Coast and Appalachian States

Directions Complete this graphic organizer to write facts and opinions about the Atlantic Coast and Appalachian states. For each main topic, write one statement of fact and one statement of opinion. Possible responses are given.

ATLANTIC COAST AND APPALACHIAN STATES

PHYSICAL FEATURES OF THE ATLANTIC COAST AND APPALACHIAN STATES

FACT:

The first colonists in the region settled along the Atlantic Coast and nearby rivers.

OPINION:

The Atlantic Ocean had the greatest effect on settlement in this region.

WAYS PEOPLE IN THE ATLANTIC COAST AND APPALACHIAN STATES USE NATURAL RESOURCES TO EARN THEIR LIVING

FACT:

Agriculture is a major industry in this region.

OPINION:

Agriculture is the best industry in this region.

REASONS WHY CITIES HAVE GROWN AND OCCUPATIONS HAVE CHANGED IN THE ATLANTIC COAST AND APPALACHIAN STATES

FACT:

Many people in this region work for governments in capital cities.

OPINION:

Cities are better places to live and work than rural areas.

PURPOSES OF NATIONAL PARKS

FACT:

Great Smoky Mountains National Park protects trees, plants, and animals.

OPINION:

Great Smoky Mountains National Park is the most beautiful park in the world.

© Harcourt

Use after reading Chapter 5, pages 168–195.

Name _____ Date _____

5 Test Preparation

Directions Read each question and choose the best answer. Then fill in the circle for the answer you have chosen. Be sure to fill in the circle completely.

1 The first attempt by the English to settle in the Atlantic Coast and Appalachian region took place—
Ⓐ along the Mississippi River.
Ⓑ on Roanoke Island.
Ⓒ on the Cumberland Plateau.
Ⓓ along the James River.

2 Which of the following is not a mountain range in the Atlantic Coast and Appalachian region?
Ⓕ Allegheny Mountains
Ⓖ Blue Ridge Mountains
Ⓗ Rocky Mountains
Ⓙ Great Smoky Mountains

3 Why does land often erode after strip mines are used?
Ⓐ because trees and grasses are removed to mine the coal
Ⓑ because most of the coal is used to produce electricity
Ⓒ because deep shafts are dug miles underground
Ⓓ because large amounts of coal are needed to produce steel

4 Which of these Atlantic Coast and Appalachian cities grew because of state government?
Ⓕ Memphis, Tennessee
Ⓖ Louisville, Kentucky
Ⓗ Chapel Hill, North Carolina
Ⓙ Richmond, Virginia

5 Which of the following is **not** a purpose of national parks?
Ⓐ to preserve cultural and historical sites
Ⓑ to clear more land for farms and industries
Ⓒ to preserve natural resources
Ⓓ to protect habitats for special wildlife

© Harcourt

Settlement and Early Life

Directions The table below compares the North with the South in 1860.
Use the information in the table to answer the questions that follow.

North and South Regions, 1860		
	NORTH	**SOUTH**
Total Population	about 20 million	about 11 million
Enslaved Population	about 100,000	about 4 million
Number of Farms of 1,000 Acres or More	about 900	about 4,400
Number of Cities with More than 1 Million People	77	16
Number of Factories	about 110,000	about 27,000
Number of Factory Workers	about 1,150,000	about 160,000
Annual Value of Factory Products	about $1,660,000,000	about $220,000,000

SOURCE: U.S. Census Bureau

1 List three details from the table that support the idea that there was more
manufacturing in the North than in the South.

The North had more factories than the South had.

The North had more factory workers than the South had.

The annual value of factory products was greater in the North than in the South.

2 What information in the table supports the idea that there were more

plantations in the South than in the North? The South had many more large

farms and slaves than the North had.

3 Use the facts in the table to make three general statements comparing the
population of the North with the population of the South in 1860.

About twice as many people lived in the North as in the South in 1860.

Many more slaves lived in the South than in the North.

More people lived in cities in the North than in the South.

Use after reading Chapter 6, Lesson 1, pages 200–205.

The Southeast and Gulf States Today

Directions Read about how cloth is made from cotton. Then write the numbers from 1 to 8 in the blanks below to put the steps in the correct order.

When cotton is ready to be picked, workers in the fields treat the plants with chemicals to remove the leaves. Then they use farm machines to pick the cotton.

Trucks bring the picked cotton to a processing plant, called a cotton gin. Machines there dry the raw cotton fibers and remove any leaves or other trash. Another machine, called a gin stand, separates the cotton fibers, called lint, from the seeds. Then the lint is cleaned.

A bale press packs the cotton into 500-pound (227-kg) bales, wraps each bale with cloth, and binds it with steel bands. Trucks carry the refrigerator-sized bales to the warehouse. There they are compressed, or squeezed, to about half their size to save space for shipping.

Government inspectors grade samples of the cotton. Growers then sell the graded cotton to brokers, or traders. Brokers, in turn, sell it to cloth manufacturers, who buy large amounts of cotton fiber for their textile factories.

When the cotton arrives at the textile factory, the bales are broken open, and machines clean the lint again and roll it into a long sheet. Then spinning machines separate and straighten the cotton fibers. Other machines twist the fibers into fine, strong thread.

Mechanical looms weave the thread into cloth. Then the cloth is dyed, or colored. Sometimes it is printed, or stamped with a pattern. The cloth manufacturer then sells the finished cotton cloth to clothing manufacturers, who cut and sew the cloth to make items of clothing.

A. ___8___ The cloth is dyed and printed.

B. ___7___ Mechanical looms weave the cotton thread into cloth.

C. ___1___ Chemicals remove the leaves from the plants, and the cotton is picked.

D. ___3___ The cotton is packed into 500-pound (227-kg) bales.

E. ___4___ Cloth manufacturers buy the cotton from brokers.

F. ___5___ Spinning machines separate and straighten the cotton fibers.

G. ___2___ At the cotton gin, the cotton lint is separated from the seeds.

H. ___6___ The cotton fibers are twisted into fine, strong thread.

MAP AND GLOBE SKILLS

Compare Maps with Different Scales

Many of the Civil War's major battles were fought in the Southeast and Gulf states. Early in the war, the Confederates won several important victories. By 1863, however, the Union was winning more battles. One of the Union's most important victories came at Vicksburg, Mississippi. Union guns pounded the city for weeks before the Confederate army surrendered. With this victory, the Union gained control of the Mississippi River. The next year, the Union army marched south from Tennessee into Georgia. After capturing and burning Atlanta, Georgia, the army continued toward Savannah, destroying nearly everything in its path. This march became known as the March to the Sea.

Directions **Use the maps on page 57 to answer the following questions.**

1 About how many miles was the Union army's March to the Sea? About how

many kilometers? _about 200 miles; about 300 kilometers_____

2 Which map would you use to find the distance between Vicksburg, Mississippi,

and Atlanta, Georgia? _Map B_____

3 About how many miles separate Vicksburg and Jackson, Mississippi? Which

map did you use to answer this question? _about 40 miles; Map A_____

4 Was the Battle of Vicksburg fought in Union or Confederate territory? Which

map did you use to answer this question? _Confederate territory; Map B_____

5 How do you think the uses of Map A compare to the uses of Map B?

Answers will vary but should show an understanding of when and why a larger or

smaller map scale would be useful. For example, if a person wanted to study all

of the major Civil War battles, he or she would want to use a larger-scale map,

such as Map B. To see more details of a specific battle, a person would want to

use a smaller-scale map, such as Map A.

(continued)

© Harcourt

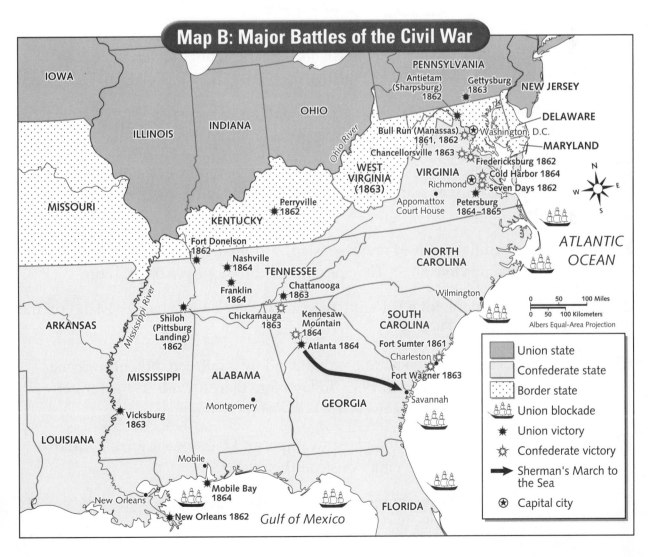

Map A: Battle of Vicksburg, 1863

Vicksburg, Shreveport & Texas R.R.

Vanguard Leaves Milliken's Bend March 31

Haynes' Bluff

Snyder's Bluff

MISSISSIPPI

New Orleans, Jackson & Great Northern R.R.

Richmond

Duckport

VICKSBURG

Battle of the Big Black River Bridge May 17

Southern R.R. of Mississippi

Clinton

Jackson

Bayou Macon

Siege of Vicksburg May 18–July 4

Edwards Station

Battle of Champion Hill May 16

Raymond

Battle of Jackson May 14

Mississippi River

LOUISIANA

Brierfield

Big Black River

Battle of Raymond May 12

Pearl River

Tensas River

Arrives at Hard Times April 28

Hard Times

Union Fleet Bombards Grand Gulf April 29

Big Bayou Pierre

Grand Gulf

Crosses Mississippi River at Bruinsburg March 31

Bruinsburg

Port Gibson

Little Bayou Pierre

Battle of Port Gibson May 1

→ Grant's march

〰 Confederate defenses

0 · 10 · 20 Miles
0 · 10 · 20 Kilometers

Map B: Major Battles of the Civil War

IOWA

ILLINOIS · **INDIANA** · **OHIO**

PENNSYLVANIA

Antietam (Sharpsburg) 1862

Gettysburg 1863

NEW JERSEY

DELAWARE

Bull Run (Manassas) 1861, 1862

Washington, D.C.

MARYLAND

Chancellorsville 1863

Fredericksburg 1862

WEST VIRGINIA (1863)

VIRGINIA

Richmond

Cold Harbor 1864

Seven Days 1862

MISSOURI

Perryville 1862

KENTUCKY

Appomattox Court House

Petersburg 1864–1865

ATLANTIC OCEAN

Fort Donelson 1862

Nashville 1864

TENNESSEE

NORTH CAROLINA

Franklin 1864

Chattanooga 1863

Wilmington

0 · 50 · 100 Miles
0 · 50 · 100 Kilometers
Albers Equal-Area Projection

ARKANSAS

Shiloh (Pittsburg Landing) 1862

Chickamauga 1863

Kennesaw Mountain 1864

SOUTH CAROLINA

Atlanta 1864

Fort Sumter 1861

Charleston

MISSISSIPPI · **ALABAMA**

Montgomery

GEORGIA

Fort Wagner 1863

Savannah

Vicksburg 1863

LOUISIANA

Mobile

Mobile Bay 1864

New Orleans

New Orleans 1862

Gulf of Mexico

FLORIDA

▨ Union state

☐ Confederate state

⠐ Border state

⛵ Union blockade

✹ Union victory

✸ Confederate victory

➤ Sherman's March to the Sea

✪ Capital city

© Harcourt

Islands and People

Directions Read the islanders' descriptions of their homes. Then write the letter of the correct island or islands in the blank next to each description. Some letters may be used more than once.

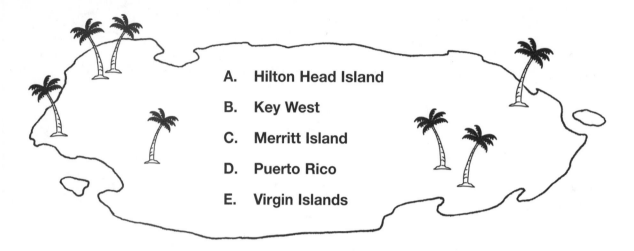

A. Hilton Head Island

B. Key West

C. Merritt Island

D. Puerto Rico

E. Virgin Islands

1 ___D___ "The language of my home island is Spanish, but I am an American citizen. My island's name means 'Rich Port' in Spanish."

2 ___A___ "I work in a hotel on this barrier island off the coast of South Carolina. It is a popular vacation resort, especially for golfers."

3 ___B___ "My home is one of the coral islands that lie off the coast of Florida. I work as a diver searching for shipwrecks along the reefs surrounding the island."

4 ___E___ "My family has lived on these islands for many years. I live on St. Croix, my parents live on St. Thomas, and my brother lives on St. John."

5 ___C___ "I work at the John F. Kennedy Space Center on this barrier island off the east coast of Florida."

6 ___B___ "My island was linked to the mainland by a railroad, but a hurricane destroyed the tracks in 1935. Today more than 100 miles (160 km) of overseas highway connects my home and the mainland."

7 ___D___ "Mountains, valleys, beaches, swamps, and rain forests are all within a day's car ride from my house on this island."

8 ___E___ "The United States purchased my islands from Denmark in 1917, and we have been a United States territory ever since."

Use after reading Chapter 6, Lesson 3, pages 214–219.

© Harcourt

Coastal Regions Around the World

Directions Number the countries in this table from 1 through 10 to put their coastlines in order from longest (1) to shortest (10). Locate each of those countries on the world map on page 60. Then complete the activities at the bottom of this page.

World's Longest Coastlines		
RANK	COUNTRY	LENGTH (in miles)
6	Australia	16,007
1	Canada	151,485
10	Brazil	4,655
2	Indonesia	33,999
5	Japan	18,486
9	New Zealand	9,404
7	Norway	13,624
4	Philippines	22,559
3	Russia	23,396
8	United States	12,380

SOURCE: *CIA Factbook*

1 Write each country's coastline rank number at its location on the map.
Check students' maps.

2 Use the map to find which countries listed in the table border the Atlantic Ocean. Shade those countries blue.
Students should shade Canada, the United States, Brazil, and Norway.

3 Use a different color to shade those countries that are an island or that are made up entirely of several islands. Students should shade Australia, Indonesia, Japan, the Philippines, and New Zealand.

4 Write **X** on the countries that are located in North America.
On the map, students should write **X** on the United States and Canada.

5 Write **Y** on the countries that border both the Indian Ocean and the Pacific Ocean. On the map, students should write **Y** on Indonesia and Australia.

(continued)

Major Coastal Countries of the World

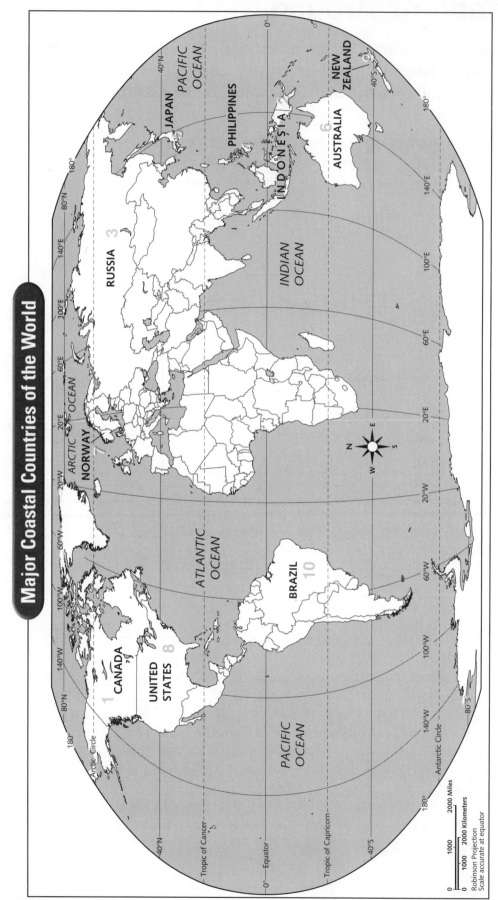

Use after reading Chapter 6, Lesson 4, pages 220–225.

Southeast and Gulf States

Directions Complete this graphic organizer to compare and contrast the Southeast and Gulf states.

Possible responses are given.

THE SOUTHEAST AND GULF STATES

Southeast States   **Gulf States**

DIFFERENCES

1. Appalachian Mountains in the western part

2. barrier islands made up of sand, soil, and shells

3. crops: peanuts, peaches

4. industries: manufacturing, mining

SIMILARITIES

1. rivers, harbors

2. islands along the coasts

3. agriculture very important

4. growing industries

DIFFERENCES

1. mostly on the Coastal Plain

2. Florida Keys made of coral

3. crops: citrus fruits, sugarcane

4. main industry: tourism

Use after reading Chapter 6, pages 198–225.

Name _____ Date _____

Test Preparation

Directions Read each question and choose the best answer. Then fill in the circle for the answer you have chosen. Be sure to fill in the circle completely.

1 Which European country was the first to claim land in the Southeast and Gulf region?
- Ⓐ England
- Ⓑ France
- Ⓒ Spain
- Ⓓ Holland

2 Why is cotton a major crop in the Southeast and Gulf region?
- Ⓕ because the region has a long growing season and plentiful rainfall
- Ⓖ because the region borders the Atlantic Ocean
- Ⓗ because the Mississippi River forms the region's western boundary
- Ⓙ because farming is the largest industry in the region

3 The Florida Keys are made up of—
- Ⓐ the peaks of mountain ranges.
- Ⓑ layers of coral and limestone.
- Ⓒ sand, shells, and soil.
- Ⓓ rain forests and swamps.

4 Which of the following is a major port city along the Gulf of Mexico?
- Ⓕ Miami, Florida
- Ⓖ Charleston, South Carolina
- Ⓗ Mobile, Alabama
- Ⓙ Savannah, Georgia

5 Which of the following countries around the world does not have coastal regions?
- Ⓐ Greece
- Ⓑ Brazil
- Ⓒ Switzerland
- Ⓓ India

© Harcourt

Use after reading Chapter 6, pages 198–225.

Settling the South Central Region

In 1830 the United States government passed the Indian Removal Act. This act said that all Native Americans living east of the Mississippi River must leave their lands and move west to the Indian Territory, in what is today Oklahoma. Many tribes fought against the removal, but by 1838, soldiers had forced nearly all of the Indians off their lands. More than 4,000 Cherokees died of cold, disease, and lack of food during their 116-day march to the Indian Territory. The Cherokees called their long, painful journey the "Trail Where They Cried." It later became known as the Trail of Tears.

Directions **Use the map to answer the following questions.**

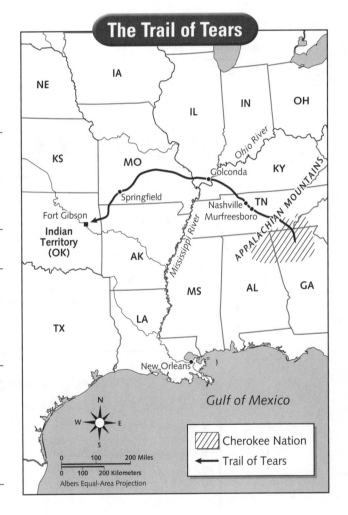

The Trail of Tears

1 In which present-day state did the Trail of Tears end?

Oklahoma

2 Through which present-day states were the Cherokees forced to march?

Georgia, Tennessee, Kentucky, Illinois, Missouri, Arkansas, and Oklahoma

3 What rivers did they have to cross during the journey?

Mississippi River and Ohio River

4 Why do you think this event in American history is known as the Trail of Tears?

Answers will vary but should show

an understanding of the sadness

Native Americans must have experienced at being forced to leave their homes

and move to unknown lands. Responses may also include the fact that they suf-

fered greatly and so many died during the forced march.

Use after reading Chapter 7, Lesson 1, pages 230–235.

© Harcourt

A Diverse Economy

Directions The table below shows the amount of exports and imports that each of the nation's five busiest ports handles each year. Use the information in the table to complete the two bar graphs that follow.

Busiest Ports in the United States		
PORT	IMPORTS (in tons per year)	EXPORTS (in tons per year)
Port of South Louisiana, LA	30,602,117	57,419,203
Houston, TX	75,118,513	33,431,259
New York, NY and NJ	53,518,545	8,028,061
New Orleans, LA	26,383,831	21,731,316
Corpus Christi, TX	52,595,352	7,635,218

SOURCE: *World Almanac, 2001*

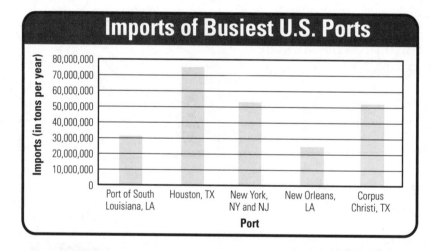

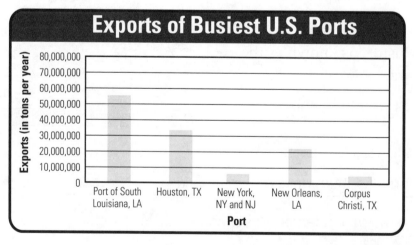

Use after reading Chapter 7, Lesson 2, pages 236–241.

© Harcourt

Sharing a River

Directions The United States–Mexico border extends about 2,067 miles (3,326 km) across North America. As a result, the two countries share many physical features. Use the map below to answer the questions that follow.

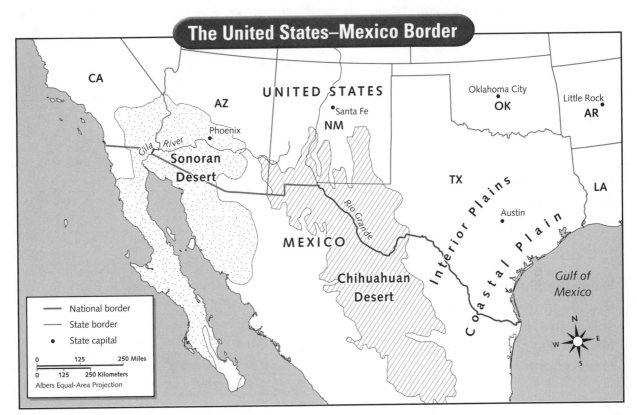

The United States–Mexico Border

1 What two major rivers do the United States and Mexico share?

Rio Grande and Gila River

2 What two large desert regions cover parts of both Mexico and the United States? Which of those deserts covers part of the South Central region?

Sonoran Desert and Chihuahuan Desert; Chihuahuan Desert

3 What two plains regions extend from the South Central states into Mexico?

Coastal Plain and Interior Plains

4 What major body of water forms the eastern boundary of Mexico and the southeastern boundary of the South Central region of the United States?

Gulf of Mexico

CITIZENSHIP SKILLS
Resolve Conflicts

Directions Sharing the Rio Grande has caused several conflicts over the years. Some of those conflicts are described below. For each conflict, describe how the two sides compromised and worked together to resolve the conflict. Possible responses are given.

CONFLICT	RESOLUTION
The riverbed of the Rio Grande was sometimes dry in Texas. People in Texas blamed people living upstream in Colorado and New Mexico for using too much of the river's water.	The United States government built several dams across the Rio Grande to make sure there was enough water downstream so that all of the states could share the river.
When the channel of the Rio Grande moved south in the 1860s, the United States and Mexico disagreed about their shared border.	The United States gave El Chamizal back to Mexico, and Mexico gave the United States some land on the north side of the Rio Grande's original channel. Both countries agreed that the Rio Grande is their official border.
Millions of people in Mexico depend on the Rio Grande for water. The way the river is used upstream in the United States affects Mexico's use of the river.	The United States and Mexico worked together to build dams and reservoirs along the Rio Grande. The United States agreed that a certain amount of the Rio Grande's water must reach Mexico.
Economic development and population growth along the Rio Grande in both Mexico and the United States increased pollution in the river.	The United States and Mexico both passed laws against dumping harmful wastes into the Rio Grande, and both are planning to build new wastewater treatment plants in towns along the river. The United States set aside land for national parks and recreation areas along the river and named the Rio Grande an American Heritage River.

© Harcourt

Use after reading Chapter 7, Skill Lesson, page 247.

Oil Resources Around the World

Millions of years ago, oceans covered even more of Earth's surface than they do today. As tiny sea creatures died, their remains sank to the bottoms of the oceans. Over time, the mud and sand that covered the creatures hardened into rock. These layers of rock pressed down on the sea creatures' remains, turning them into oil. In fact, much of the world's oil lies buried hundreds of feet below the surface of the ocean. To reach and remove this oil, people build offshore oil rigs.

Directions **The drawing on page 68 is a cross-section diagram of an offshore oil rig. It shows what you would see if you could slice through the ocean and then look at the cut surface. Use the diagram to answer the following questions about how an offshore oil rig works.**

1 What parts of an offshore oil rig hold the derrick and other equipment above the ocean water?

the platform and steel legs

2 What materials make up the layers separating the ocean waters from the oil deposits? Which of those materials is a fuel resource?

sand, porous rock, nonporous rock, and natural gas; natural gas

3 What equipment digs a hole through those layers to reach the oil?

the drill pipe and rotary bit

4 Where on the offshore rig does the oil go after it is brought up through pipes from the ocean floor?

into storage tanks on the platform

5 How does the oil get from the offshore oil rig to refineries on the mainland?

It is pumped into oil tankers, which carry the oil to the mainland.

6 How do you think workers get to their jobs on offshore oil rigs?

Answers will vary but most students will say the workers ride boats or helicopters

to the offshore oil rigs.

(continued)

© Harcourt

Name _____ Date _____

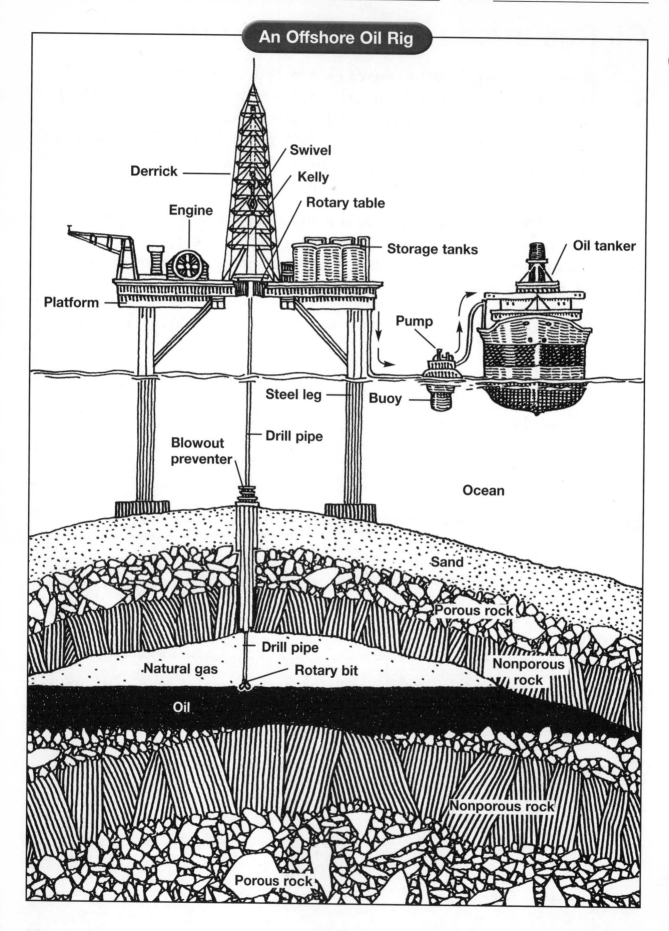

An Offshore Oil Rig

Swivel
Derrick
Kelly
Engine
Rotary table
Storage tanks
Oil tanker
Platform
Pump
Steel leg
Buoy
Drill pipe
Blowout
preventer
Ocean
Sand
Porous rock
Nonporous
rock
Drill pipe
Natural gas
Rotary bit
Oil
Nonporous rock
Porous rock

© Harcourt

Use after reading Chapter 7, Lesson 4, pages 248–251.

South Central States

Directions Use this graphic organizer to categorize information about the South Central states. Complete it by listing two facts for each subject category.

Possible responses are given.

GEOGRAPHY

1. The Rio Grande and the Gulf of Mexico form the southern boundary of the region.

2. The Coastal Plain covers all of Louisiana, eastern Texas, and southern Arkansas.

HISTORY

1. Spanish and French explorers were the first Europeans to claim land in the region.

2. Much of the region became part of the United States with the Louisiana Purchase in 1803.

SOUTH CENTRAL STATES

ECONOMY

1. Until the early 1900s, most people in the South Central region worked on farms or ranches.

2. Today the region has a diverse economy.

CULTURE

1. Many people living in the South Central region, especially in Texas, have Hispanic ancestors.

2. Much of southern Louisiana has a unique French heritage.

Use after reading Chapter 7, pages 228–251.

Name _____ Date _____

7 Test Preparation

Directions Read each question and choose the best answer. Then fill in the circle for the answer you have chosen. Be sure to fill in the circle completely.

1 Near what present-day city did Spanish colonists from Mexico build their first settlement in the South Central region?
- Ⓐ New Orleans, Louisiana
- Ⓑ Houston, Texas
- Ⓒ El Paso, Texas
- Ⓓ Tulsa, Oklahoma

2 Many bayous are located in the—
- Ⓕ Ozark Plateau.
- Ⓖ Chihuahuan Desert.
- Ⓗ Great Plains.
- Ⓙ Mississippi Delta.

3 Why did early Texas ranchers drive their cattle north to towns in Missouri, Kansas, and Nebraska?
- Ⓐ to reach better grazing land
- Ⓑ to ship the cattle to markets on railroads
- Ⓒ to trade for horses at larger ranches
- Ⓓ to reach rivers so their cattle would have drinking water

4 Which of the following industries is *not* a major part of the South Central region's diverse economy?
- Ⓕ mining silver and gold
- Ⓖ shipping and trading goods
- Ⓗ drilling and refining oil
- Ⓙ growing cotton and rice

5 The world's leading producer of oil is—
- Ⓐ Nigeria.
- Ⓑ Russia.
- Ⓒ Saudi Arabia.
- Ⓓ the United States.

© Harcourt

Use after reading Chapter 7, pages 228–251.

The Old Northwest

Directions The following excerpt is from *Abraham Lincoln: A First Book* by Larry Metzger. It describes what life was like for settlers moving to the Northwest Territory. Read the excerpt. Then answer the questions that follow.

Moving on the frontier was a difficult business. The Lincolns walked the entire way, because they carried things like pots, pans, and a spinning wheel on their horses and in their wagon. They traveled over 100 miles (160 km) on foot, crossing the mighty Ohio River and cutting their way through the heavy forest on the other side....

Winter was a bad time to be settling into a new home in the wilderness.... The Lincolns had to build some kind of shelter quickly.... Thomas [Lincoln's father] was a skilled carpenter who had built several cabins before, and Abraham was able to help by clearing brush and by trimming branches from the logs that were used to make the cabin walls.... The Lincolns heated their home by burning wood in a stone fireplace, and they filled the spaces between the logs with mud and grass in order to keep out the wind....

When spring came that year, it was time for the family to clear the trees and brush so they could start a farm. This was hard work, because the land was heavily wooded and they had only axes to do the job. Even though Abraham was only eight years old, he helped his father chop down trees and split logs for firewood and fence rails.

After they cleared the land, Abraham and his father plowed the soil and planted corn. When the corn ripened, Abraham helped harvest it and carry it to the mill, where it was ground into flour.

From *Abraham Lincoln: A First Book* by Larry Metzger. Text copyright © 1987 by Larry Metzger. Reprinted by permission of Franklin Watts, a Division of Grolier Publishing.

1 How did the Lincolns reach their new home in the Northwest Territory?

They walked there and used horses and a wagon to carry their supplies.

2 What natural resources did the Lincolns use for their new home? trees for the walls of the cabin and mud and grass to fill in the spaces between the logs; stones to build their fireplace; and wood for fences

3 What kind of work did Abraham do to help his family survive on the frontier?

He helped build the family's cabin, chopped wood, and worked on the family's farm.

Name _____ Date _____

MAP AND GLOBE SKILLS
Compare Historical Maps

Directions The French and Indian War began in 1754 and ended in 1763. The two historical maps below show the different countries that claimed land in North America before and after the war. Use the maps to answer the questions.

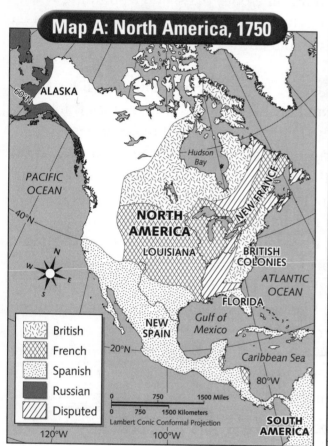

1. Which country claimed more land in North America in 1763, the British or the French? the British

2. How did Spanish claims to land in North America change after the French and Indian War? Spain gained much of the French lands west of the Mississippi River, but it lost control of Florida to the British.

3. How did the French and Indian War affect control of the Great Lakes region? Before the French and Indian War, most of the Great Lakes region was claimed by France. After the war, most of the region was claimed by Britain.

Use after reading Chapter 8, Skill Lesson, pages 274–275.

© Harcourt

Life in the Great Lakes Region

Directions Use the information in this table about the Great Lakes to answer the questions that follow.

Facts about the Great Lakes					
LAKE	**Erie**	**Huron**	**Michigan**	**Ontario**	**Superior**
ORIGIN OF NAME	Iroquois Indian for "cat"	Huron Indians	Ojibwa Indian for "great lake"	Iroquois for "beautiful lake"	French for "greatest"
AREA in square miles (sq km)	9,910 (25,667)	23,000 (59,570)	22,400 (58,016)	7,600 (19,684)	31,800 (82,362)
BORDERS	Michigan, New York, Ohio, Pennsylvania, Canada	Michigan, Canada	Illinois, Indiana, Michigan, Wisconsin	New York, Canada	Michigan, Minnesota, Wisconsin, Canada
MAJOR U.S. PORTS	Buffalo, Cleveland, Erie, Toledo	Bay City, Port Huron	Chicago, Gary, Milwaukee	Oswego, Rochester	Duluth, Superior

1 Which Great Lakes names originate from Native American languages?

Erie, Huron, Michigan, and Ontario

2 What is the largest Great Lake? the smallest?

Lake Superior; Lake Ontario

3 What is the only Great Lake that does *not* border any of the Great Lakes states?

Lake Ontario

4 What are some major port cities along Lake Michigan?

Chicago, Gary, and Milwaukee

River Transportation

Directions This map shows some of the towns and cities that grew up along rivers in the Middle West region of the United States. Study the map. Then answer the questions that follow.

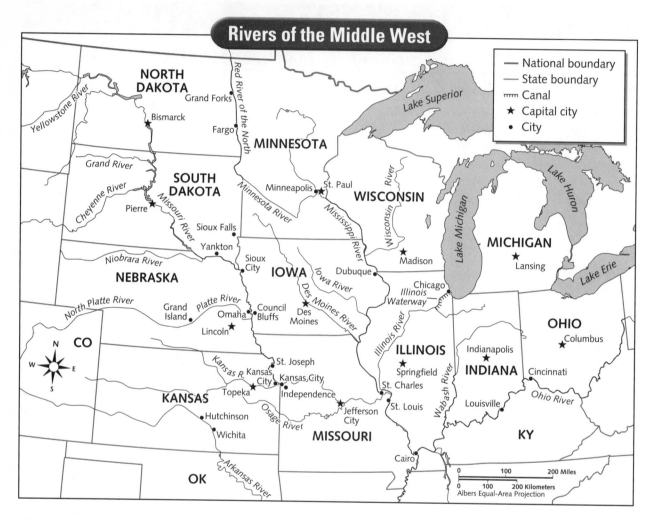

Rivers of the Middle West

1 Which capital cities in the Middle West region are located along rivers?

St. Paul, Des Moines, Jefferson City, Bismarck, Pierre, and Topeka

2 Which river forms part of the border between Illinois and Indiana?

the Wabash River

3 Into what large river does the Platte River flow? the Missouri River

(continued)

Use after reading Chapter 8, Lesson 3, pages 281–285.

4 Imagine that you are traveling by river in the Middle West region. According to the map, which river or rivers could you use if you were going from

a. Cincinnati, Ohio, to St. Louis, Missouri?

the Ohio River and the Mississippi River

b. St. Joseph, Kansas, to Sioux City, Iowa?

the Missouri River

c. Chicago, Illinois, to Cairo, Illinois?

the Illinois River and the Mississippi River

d. Minneapolis, Minnesota, to Des Moines, Iowa?

the Mississippi River and the Des Moines River

5 What are two tributaries of the Missouri River that flow through South Dakota?

the Grand River and Cheyenne River

6 Which rivers in the Middle West region share their names with Middle West states? the Ohio River, Illinois River, Minnesota River, Missouri River, Kansas River, Wisconsin River, and Iowa River

7 Which two Middle West states have cities named Kansas City? What two rivers meet near those two cities? Kansas and Missouri; the Kansas River and the Missouri River

8 How are boats from Lake Michigan able to reach rivers in the Middle West region? by using the Illinois Waterway and the Illinois River

_____

Name _____ Date _____

Rivers Around the World

Directions Read the sentences below about rivers around the world. Then select the words from the boats to correctly complete each sentence.

1 The ____Nile River____ is the most important source of fresh water in Egypt.

2 A tropical location and high precipitation levels have produced the world's

   largest ____rain forest____ along the ____Amazon River____.

3 For Hindus, the ____Ganges River____ is a holy river.

4 Farmers in China grow tons of rice in ____paddies____ stretching from the

   banks of the ____Chang Jiang____.

5 The ____Aswan High Dam____ stops the Nile River from flooding and supplies fresh
   water and electricity for people and industries.

6 From its ____source____ in the mountains of Peru, the Amazon River flows
   east across Brazil to the Atlantic Ocean.

7 Industries in many European countries use the ____Rhine River____ to transport

   raw materials and finished products to the ocean port of ____Rotterdam____.

Use after reading Chapter 8, Lesson 4, pages 286–290.

Name _____ Date _____

CITIZENSHIP SKILLS
Make a Thoughtful Decision

Directions Think about a decision you made recently in school. Then use the graphic organizer below to record and analyze your decision-making process. Fill in as many possible actions and consequences as you can.

GOAL

_____
_____
_____
_____

POSSIBLE ACTIONS

1 _____
2 _____
3 _____
4 _____

POSSIBLE CONSEQUENCES

1 _____
2 _____
3 _____
4 _____

YOUR CHOICE

_____
_____
_____
_____

REASONS FOR YOUR CHOICE

_____
_____
_____
_____

THE RESULT OF YOUR CHOICE

_____
_____
_____

Students' responses should demonstrate an ability to analyze decisions. Look for answers that illustrate the relationship between possible actions and consequences and that show evidence of a thoughtful decision-making process.

© Harcourt

Use after reading Chapter 8, Skill Lesson, page 291.

Activity Book ▪ 77

Name _____   Date _____

Great Lakes States

Directions Use this graphic organizer to sequence events that have occurred in the Great Lakes states. Complete it by writing the event in the appropriate date's box. Possible responses are given.

GREAT LAKES STATES

1673

Marquette and Joliet begin their expedition to find and explore the Mississippi River.

1787

The Northwest Ordinance of 1787 sets up a plan for governing the Northwest Territory and describes the steps for statehood there.

1812

The War of 1812 between Britain and the United States begins; the steamboat *New Orleans* travels the Mississippi River system.

1820s

Steamboats become one of the main forms of transportation in the United States.

1858

All of the Great Lakes states have been admitted into the United States.

1913

Henry Ford opens his first auto assembly line in Detroit.

© Harcourt

Use after reading Chapter 8, pages 266–291.

Name _____ Date _____

8 Test Preparation

Directions Read each question and choose the best answer. Then fill in the circle for the answer you have chosen. Be sure to fill in the circle completely.

1 After which war did the United States gain control of most of the Great Lakes region?

Ⓐ the American Revolution

Ⓑ the Civil War

Ⓒ the French and Indian War

Ⓓ the War of 1812

2 The Northwest Territory was divided into squares called—

Ⓕ ordinances.

Ⓖ townships.

Ⓗ territories.

Ⓙ frontiers.

3 Which of the following is *not* a major reason why the automobile industry grew in the Great Lakes region?

Ⓐ The region has many navigable waterways to ship goods.

Ⓑ Factory owners in the region used mass production to produce cars.

Ⓒ The region's steel industry provided materials needed to manufacture cars.

Ⓓ People buy more cars in this region than anywhere else in the country.

4 On what kind of boats are most goods shipped on the Mississippi River today?

Ⓕ barges

Ⓖ steamboats

Ⓗ flatboats

Ⓙ keelboats

5 Along which river would you see miles and miles of rice paddies?

Ⓐ the Ganges River

Ⓑ the Chang Jiang

Ⓒ the Amazon River

Ⓓ the Nile River

Use after reading Chapter 8, pages 266–291.

Name _____   Date _____

Early Days on the Interior Plains

Directions The following excerpt is from *Frontier Living* by Edwin Tunis. Read the excerpt. Then complete the activities that follow.

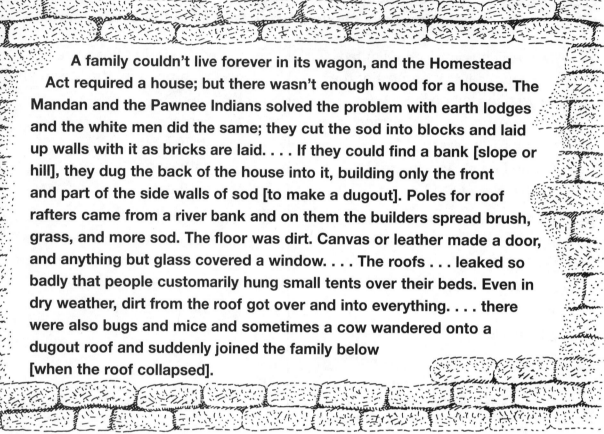

A family couldn't live forever in its wagon, and the Homestead Act required a house; but there wasn't enough wood for a house. The Mandan and the Pawnee Indians solved the problem with earth lodges and the white men did the same; they cut the sod into blocks and laid up walls with it as bricks are laid. . . . If they could find a bank [slope or hill], they dug the back of the house into it, building only the front and part of the side walls of sod [to make a dugout]. Poles for roof rafters came from a river bank and on them the builders spread brush, grass, and more sod. The floor was dirt. Canvas or leather made a door, and anything but glass covered a window. . . . The roofs . . . leaked so badly that people customarily hung small tents over their beds. Even in dry weather, dirt from the roof got over and into everything. . . . there were also bugs and mice and sometimes a cow wandered onto a dugout roof and suddenly joined the family below [when the roof collapsed].

From *Frontier Living* by Edwin Tunis. Text copyright © 1961 by Edwin Tunis. Published by HarperCollins Publishers. Reprinted by permission of Curtis Brown, Ltd.

1 Why did pioneers on the Great Plains build sod houses? There was not enough wood on the Great Plains to build a house, and the Homestead Act required that settlers build a house.

2 List the steps a pioneer family followed to build a sod house. They cut sod into blocks and laid up walls, using the sod like bricks. Then they made roof rafters from poles and spread brush, grass, and more sod on them. Finally, they made a door from canvas or leather.

3 On a separate sheet of paper, describe how you would feel if you lived in a sod house. How would living in such a house be different from where you live today? What are some items in your home that you would find it difficult to live without in a sod house? Responses should reflect students' interpretation of the description in the excerpt.

© Harcourt

80 ▪ **Activity Book**   Use after reading Chapter 9, Lesson 1, pages 296–301.

Name _____ Date _____

MAP AND GLOBE SKILLS
Use a Cultural Map

Directions Use the map on page 82 to answer the questions below.

1 Which Native American cultural groups labeled on the map
lived in what is now called the Plains region of the United States?

Mandan, Sioux, Cheyenne, Pawnee, Arapaho, Kaw, Osage, Missouri, and Iowa

2 What tribes labeled on the map lived along the shores of the Great Lakes?

Ojibwa, Chippewa, Sauk, Fox, Illinois, Miami, Erie, Huron, Ottawa, and the Iroquois

League—Cayuga, Mohawk, Oneida, Onondaga, and Seneca

3 How do you think life for Caribbean Native American groups differed from life
for Arctic Native American groups? Answers will vary but students should
compare living in a tropical climate to living in an arctic climate and show an
understanding of how environments affect life.

4 In what present-day country did the Aztec Indians live? Mexico

5 Which Native American group or groups lived where your state is today?

Answers will depend on the location of the students' state but should correctly
identify the tribe or tribes labeled on the map as living in that state.

6 What connection do you see between the names of the Native American cultural
groups on the map and the names of places in the United States today?

Many cities, towns, states, and physical features in the United States have

names that are the same as or similar to the names of Native American cultural

groups.

(continued)

Use after reading Chapter 9, Skill Lesson, pages 302–303.

© Harcourt

Early Cultures of North America

ASIA

ARCTIC OCEAN

INUPIAT

YUP'IK

ALEUT

ATHABASKAN

HAN

INUIT

INUIT

INUIT

INUIT

TLINGIT

KASKA

HAIDA

CHIPEWYAN

Hudson Bay

INUIT

NASKAPI

BEOTHUK

BELLA COOLA

NOOTKA

PACIFIC OCEAN

MAKAH

CHINOOK

KOOTENAI

CREE

BLACKFOOT

CREE

CREE

CREE

MICMAC

ASSINIBOINE

OJIBWA

OJIBWA

ALGONKIN

PENOBSCOT

YAKIMA

NEZ PERCE

CROW

MANDAN

CHIPPEWA

OTTAWA

HURON

MASSACHUSET

POMO

PAIUTE

SHOSHONE

KAW

CHEYENNE

SIOUX

SIOUX

SAUK FOX

ERIE

IROQUOIS

IROQUOIS LEAGUE

CAYUGA

MOHAWK

ONEIDA

ONONDAGA

SENECA

SHOSHONE

UTE

PAWNEE

IOWA

MIAMI

DELAWARE

ARAPAHO

MISSOURI

ILLINOIS

POWHATAN

YOKUTS

CHUMASH

PAIUTE

APACHE

OSAGE

SHAWNEE

TUSCARORA

HOPI

NAVAJO

PUEBLO

ACOMA

ZUNI

TOHO'NO-O'OTAM

APACHE

KIOWA

COMANCHE

QUAPAW

YUCHI

CHEROKEE

CADDO

CHICKASAW

CHOCTAW

NATCHEZ

ATLANTIC OCEAN

TIMUCUA

CALUSA

YAQUI

Gulf of Mexico

COAHUILTEC

HUICHOL

CIBONEY

TAINO

ARAWAK

CIBONEY

TOLTEC

AZTEC

MAYA

Carribbean Sea

MIXTEC

ZAPOTEC

MOSQUITO

SOUTH AMERICA

0   300   600 Miles
0   300   600 Kilometers
Azimuthal Equal-Area Projection

N W E S

Legend:
- Arctic
- Subarctic
- Northwest Coast
- Plateau
- California
- Great Basin
- Southwest
- Plains
- Eastern Woodlands
- Middle America
- Caribbean
- Present-day border

© Harcourt

Use after reading Chapter 9, Skill Lesson, pages 302–303.

Farming and Ranching on the Plains

Directions Read the information at the bottom of this page and on page 84 about some famous entrepreneurs in American history. Then fill in the missing information in the chart below. Use your textbook to find the information for Joseph McCoy.

Entrepreneur	Company and Product or Service It Supplied	Demand the Business Met
Joyce C. Hall	Hallmark Cards, Inc. greeting cards	inexpensive greeting cards with matching envelopes
John Harvey Kellogg	Kellogg's cereals	a softer, healthful, ready-to-eat breakfast food
Joseph McCoy	Stockyards along railroads cattle shipping and trade	a way for Texas ranchers to ship their cattle to markets and a way for people in the East to get meat
Richard W. Sears	Sears, Roebuck and Company mail-order sales	manufactured goods for sale through the mail to areas with few stores
Levi Strauss	Levi Strauss & Co. jeans	pants strong enough to last through the hard work of mining gold
Sarah Walker	Madame C. J. Walker Manufacturing Company beauty products	beauty products for African American women

Joyce C. Hall grew up in Nebraska in the late 1800s. He used money he had earned during high school to start a greeting card business in Kansas City, Missouri, in 1910. Hall helped create the modern greeting-card industry by being one of the first people to sell inexpensive cards with matching envelopes instead of the postcards and elaborate valentines common at the time. Today, Hallmark Cards, Inc., is the largest greeting-card manufacturer in the world.

(continued)

John Harvey Kellogg was an American doctor and health-food pioneer during the late 1800s. Kellogg was once sued by a woman who broke her false teeth on the hard bread that he had recommended she should eat each morning. Because of this incident, Kellogg decided to produce a softer, healthful, ready-to-eat breakfast food. The result was the world's first dry cereal, which today is known as Kellogg's Corn Flakes.

Richard W. Sears began working as a station agent for the Minneapolis and St. Louis Railway in the 1880s. While working, he saw a great demand for manufactured products in the rural Middle West, where there were few stores. So Sears started a mail-order business with his partner, Alvah C. Roebuck. With low prices, free delivery, and a great variety of products, the company grew rapidly. Today, Sears, Roebuck and Company is still one of the most successful retail sales businesses in the world.

Levi Strauss, an immigrant from Germany, left New York City for California in 1850. He made the journey west to sell canvas to settlers to use for sails and for coverings for their wagons. When Strauss arrived there, he found that settlers could not find pants strong enough to last through their hard days working in the gold mines. So Strauss took his canvas material and made it into the first pair of jeans. The company he started became Levi Strauss & Co., the world's largest pants manufacturer.

Sarah Walker was born in 1867 and grew up very poor in rural Louisiana. After moving to St. Louis, Missouri, Walker began selling her homemade beauty products door-to-door. At the time, few companies supplied such products for African American women. Her business, Madame C. J. Walker Manufacturing Company, soon employed more than 3,000 people, most of whom were African American women. Walker was the first woman to become a self-made millionaire in the United States.

© Harcourt

Name _____ Date _____

CHART AND GRAPH SKILLS
Read a Double-Bar Graph

Directions Use the double-bar graph to answer the questions.

1 Which Plains state had the highest population in 1900? in 2000?

Missouri; Missouri

2 About how many people lived in South Dakota in 1900? in 2000?

about 400,000; about

750,000

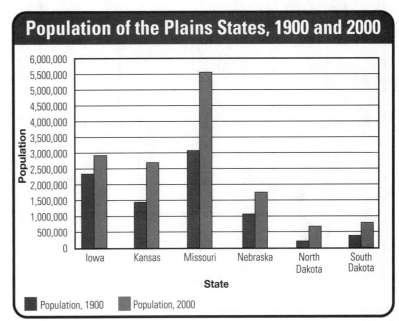

Population of the Plains States, 1900 and 2000

SOURCE: U.S. Census Bureau

3 How did the population of Nebraska in 1900 compare to its population in 2000?

Possible responses: Its population was greater in 2000 than in 1900; about

700,000 more people lived in Nebraska in 2000 than in 1900.

4 Which state's population changed less between 1900 and 2000, Iowa's or

Kansas's? Iowa's

5 Why do you think North Dakota had the lowest population of the Plains states in

both 1900 and 2000? Answers will vary but should show an understanding of North

Dakota's location and geography. It is the northernmost Plains state, so it has the

coldest climate; It lies almost entirely in the Great Plains, which have a drier climate

and less fertile land. Students should explain that because of these factors, fewer

people moved to North Dakota than to other Plains states over the years.

© Harcourt

Use after reading Chapter 9, Skill Lesson, pages 312–313.   **Activity Book ▪ 85**

Name _____ Date _____

The Plains States Today

Directions Study the two line graphs below. Then use the information on the graphs to answer the questions that follow.

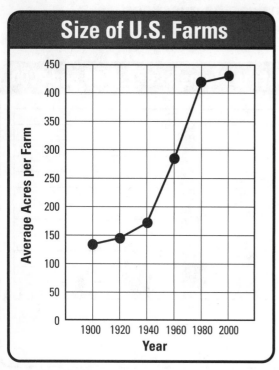

Size of U.S. Farms

SOURCE: U.S. Census Bureau

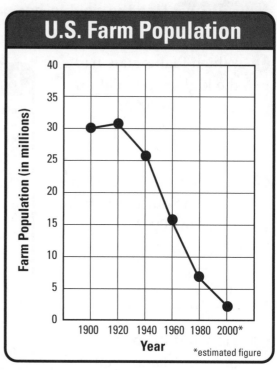

U.S. Farm Population

*estimated figure

SOURCE: U.S. Census Bureau

1 How have farms in the United States changed in the past 100 years?

They have grown larger.

2 How has the number of people who live on farms in the United States changed in the past 100 years?

The number of people who live on farms has decreased.

3 Which 20-year period shows the biggest increase in the size of farms?

between 1960 and 1980

4 About how many fewer people lived on farms in 1960 than in 1900?

about 15 million

© Harcourt

Use after reading Chapter 9, Lesson 3, pages 314–319.

Plains Around the World

Directions Read each statement below. On the line provided, write whether the statement applies to the Pampas of Argentina, the Interior Plains of the United States, or both regions.

1. The western half is much drier than the eastern half.   Both regions _____

2. It stretches all the way from Canada to Mexico.   Interior Plains _____

3. Ranches called *estancias* cover thousands of acres.   Pampas _____

4. Spanish settlers brought the first cattle and horses.   Both regions _____

5. It borders the Atlantic Ocean.   Pampas _____

6. Most early settlers here built sod houses.   Interior Plains _____

Directions Read each statement below. On the line provided, write whether the statement applies to the Nullarbor Plain of Australia, the European Plain of Poland, or both regions.

7. Many people here earn a living as farmers.   European Plain _____

8. Flat land covers most of the region.   Both regions _____

9. Sheep and cattle ranching are important industries.   Nullarbor Plain _____

10. Immigrants from here brought the first winter wheat to the United States.   European Plain _____

11. It stretches inland from a bay of the Indian Ocean.   Nullarbor Plain _____

12. The meaning of its name describes its geography.   Both regions _____

Use after reading Chapter 9, Lesson 4, pages 320–323.

Name _____ Date _____

Plains States

Directions Use this graphic organizer to draw conclusions about the Plains states. To complete it, read each listed fact. Then write any related facts you already know. Finally, draw a conclusion based on your listed facts.

PLAINS STATES

Facts I Know	New Facts	Conclusion
Possible response: Both of those states lie mostly in the Central Plains.	**Most early pioneers in the Plains region settled in Missouri or Iowa.**	Possible response: Most early settlers in the Plains region settled on the Central Plains.
Possible response: Many foods I eat every day are made with wheat and corn.	**The Plains states are large producers of wheat and corn.**	Possible response: Many foods I eat every day come from the Plains states.
Possible response: Service industries are the fastest-growing industries in many other regions of the United States today.	**Service industries are the fastest-growing industries in the Plains states today.**	Possible response: Service industries are the fastest-growing industries in the United States today.

© Harcourt

Use after reading Chapter 9, pages 294–323.

Name _____   Date _____

9 Test Preparation

Directions Read each question and choose the best answer. Then fill in the circle for the answer you have chosen. Be sure to fill in the circle completely.

1 During most of their journey to the Plains region, early pioneers traveled over miles of—
Ⓐ forests.
Ⓑ wheat fields.
Ⓒ prairie.
Ⓓ desert.

2 Which of the following is *not* a way that the Sioux adapted to their new environment on the Great Plains?
Ⓕ They lived in sod houses instead of log cabins.
Ⓖ They used horses for travel instead of canoes.
Ⓗ They hunted buffalo instead of farming the land.
Ⓙ They burned buffalo chips instead of wood.

3 What is a main difference between the Central Plains and the Great Plains?
Ⓐ The Central Plains lie farther west than the Great Plains.
Ⓑ The Central Plains get more precipitation than the Great Plains.
Ⓒ The Great Plains are more fertile than the Central Plains.
Ⓓ There are more trees on the Great Plains than on the Central Plains.

4 Which of the following do *not* usually occur in the Plains region?
Ⓕ blizzards
Ⓖ tornadoes
Ⓗ hailstorms
Ⓙ hurricanes

5 Why is meat packing a large industry in both the Plains region of the United States and the Pampas of Argentina?
Ⓐ because people in both places eat a lot of meat
Ⓑ because both places have extensive railroads
Ⓒ because cattle ranching is a large industry in both places
Ⓓ because wheat farming is a large industry in both places

© Harcourt

Use after reading Chapter 9, pages 294–323.

People and Mountains

Exhausted after a hard year of travel, Meriwether Lewis and William Clark finally reached the Rocky Mountains in the late summer of 1805. The Shoshone Indians who lived in the area warned the explorers that crossing those immense mountains would be extremely difficult. Yet Lewis and Clark had to face the challenge in order to reach the Pacific Ocean and complete their journey across North America.

Directions **While crossing the Bitterroot Range of the Rocky Mountains, Lewis and Clark continued to record their adventures in their journals. Read each of their journal entries below. Then draw a picture next to each entry to illustrate the events Lewis and Clark described.**

September 2, 1805

We set out early and proceeded... through thickets [tangled bushes] in which we were obliged to cut a road, over rocky hillsides.... With the greatest of difficulty and risk we made 7 ½ miles.

September 3, 1805

This day we passed over immense hills and some of the worst roads that ever horses passed. Our horses frequently fell. Snow about 2 inches deep when it began to rain and sleet.

© Harcourt

(continued)

Use after reading Chapter 10, Lesson 1, pages 342–347.

September 15, 1805

Four miles up the mountain. . . .
When we arrived at the top . . .
I could observe high rugged
mountains in every direction as
far as I could see.

September 18, 1805

We marched 18 miles this day
and encamped on the side of a
steep mountain . . . on a bold
running creek, which I call
Hungry Creek, as at that place
we had nothing to eat.

September 19, 1805

The ridge terminated [ended]
and we, to our inexpressible
joy, discovered a large tract
[area] of prairie country lying
to the southwest.

Students' illustrations should match the events and scenes described in each journal
entry. Look for creativity in illustrating the geography of the Rocky Mountains and the
difficulty the explorers had in crossing them.

Use after reading Chapter 10, Lesson 1, pages 342–347.

Name _____ Date _____

CHART AND GRAPH SKILLS
Read a Cutaway Diagram

Before trains linked the Mountain region to the rest of the country, stagecoaches were the only form of public transportation for travelers heading west. Although journeys by stagecoach were faster than by wagon train, they were long, rough, and uncomfortable. Coaches were usually loaded down with passengers, merchandise, luggage, and mail.

Directions Study this cutaway diagram of a stagecoach. Then answer the questions that follow.

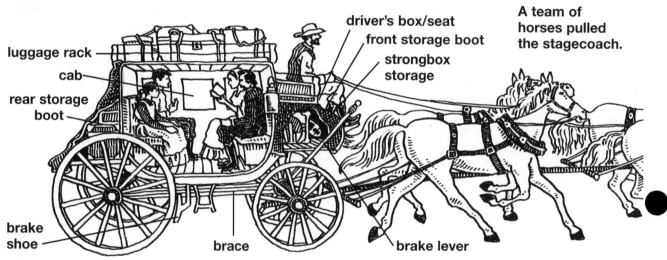

1 What parts of a stagecoach were used for storage?

the rear storage boot, the front storage boot, the luggage rack, the strongbox

2 Where did people sit in a stagecoach? Passengers sat in the cab of the stage-

coach, and the driver sat in the front of the stagecoach on the driver's box/seat.

3 How did the driver stop the stagecoach? by pulling the brake lever

4 Describe some similarities and differences between a stagecoach and a covered

wagon. Answers will vary but students should compare and contrast the diagram of the stagecoach to the diagram of the covered wagon on page 348 of their text-books. Possible similarities: Both forms of transportation were used in the 1800s to travel and carry goods to the western United States before there were railroads. Both were enclosed wagons pulled by animals. Possible differences: Stagecoaches were faster. Stagecoaches were a form of public transportation—carrying passengers—while covered wagons usually just carried the families who owned them.

Use after reading Chapter 10, Skill Lesson, pages 348–349.

The Mountain Region Today

Directions Use the maps on page 94 to answer the questions below.

1 When and where was the first national park established in the United States?

1872; Yellowstone National Park in Wyoming, Idaho, and Montana

2 Why do the Mountain states have some of the highest elevations in the West?

because the Rocky Mountains cover much of the Mountain region

3 What national park names in the West suggest that they protect mountain areas?

Answers will vary but should include any of the following: Rocky Mountain

National Park, Mount Rainier National Park, Grand Teton National Park, North

Cascades National Park.

4 What desert regions are located in the West?

Mojave Desert, Great Basin, Sonoran Desert, Painted Desert, and Chihuahuan

Desert

5 In what western state were eight national parks established in 1980?

Alaska

6 What is the elevation of the land along most of the Snake River?

1,640–6,560 ft (500–2,000 m)

7 What are some of the mountain ranges that make up the Rocky Mountains?

Teton Range, Front Range, Bitterroot Range, and Wasatch Range

8 What was the first national park established in Utah? When was it established?

Zion National Park; in 1919

© Harcourt

(continued)

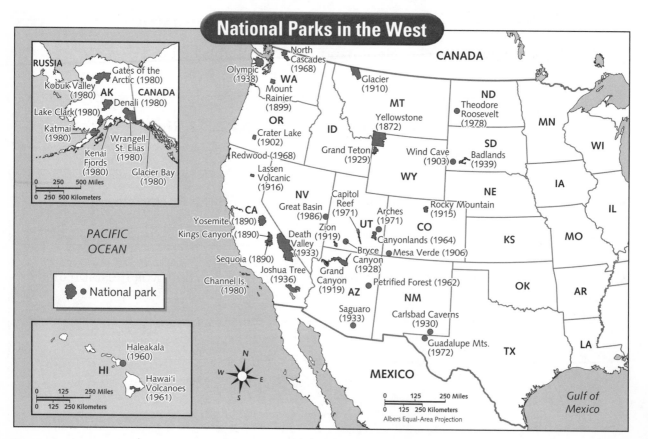

Landforms and Elevations in the West

ALASKA inset
ARCTIC OCEAN
RUSSIA
BROOKS RANGE
ALASKA   CANADA
Mt. McKinley 20,320 ft.(6,194 m)
ALASKA RANGE
Bering Sea
Kodiak Is.
Gulf of Alaska
0   250   500 Miles
0   250   500 Kilometers

ELEVATIONS
Feet   Meters
Above 13,120   Above 4,000
6,560   2,000
1,640   500
655   200
0   0
Below sea level
▲ Mountain peak
••• Continental divide

HAWAII inset
Kauai
Niihau   Oahu   Molokai
Lanai   Maui
PACIFIC OCEAN
Mauna Kea 13,796 ft. (4,205 m)   Hawaii
0   125   250 Miles
0   125   250 Kilometers

CANADA
WASHINGTON
Mt. Rainier 14,410 ft.(4,392 m)
Mt. St. Helens 8,364 ft.(2,549 m)
Columbia R.
Portland
Mt. Hood 11,235 ft.(3,427 m)
CASCADE RANGE
COAST RANGES
OREGON
Columbia Plateau
IDAHO
Boise
Snake River
BITTERROOT MTS.
MONTANA
Yellowstone River
Billings
GREAT
Missouri River
ND
SD
Teton Range
WYOMING
NE
N. Platte River
CALIFORNIA
NEVADA
GREAT BASIN
Great Salt Lake
Salt Lake City
Wasatch Range
UTAH
Green R.
Colorado River
ROCKY MOUNTAINS
Cheyenne
Front Range
Denver
Pikes Peak 14,110 ft. (4,301 m)
S. Platte River
COLORADO
Arkansas River
KS
SIERRA NEVADA
Sacramento R.
Central Valley
San Joaquin R.
COAST RANGES
San Francisco
PACIFIC OCEAN
Death Valley 282 ft. (-86 m)
Mt. Whitney 14,495 ft. (4,418 m)
Las Vegas
Painted Desert
Santa Fe
Los Angeles
MOJAVE DESERT
Salton Sea
Imperial Valley
SONORAN DESERT
ARIZONA
Phoenix
Rio Grande
NEW MEXICO
TX
CHIHUAHUAN DESERT
MEXICO
0   250   500 Miles
0   250   500 Kilometers
Albers Equal-Area Projection

National Parks in the West

ALASKA inset
RUSSIA
Gates of the Arctic (1980)
Kobuk Valley (1980)
AK   CANADA
Lake Clark (1980)   Denali (1980)
Katmai (1980)
Kenai Fjords (1980)
Wrangell–St. Elias (1980)
Glacier Bay (1980)
0   250   500 Miles
0   250   500 Kilometers

PACIFIC OCEAN

● National park

HAWAII inset
Haleakala (1960)
HI
Hawai'i Volcanoes (1961)
0   125   250 Miles
0   125   250 Kilometers

North Cascades (1968)
Olympic (1938)
WA
Mount Rainier (1899)
OR
Crater Lake (1902)
Redwood (1968)
Lassen Volcanic (1916)
CA
Yosemite (1890)
Kings Canyon (1890)
Sequoia (1890)
Channel Is. (1980)
Joshua Tree (1936)
CANADA
Glacier (1910)
MT
Yellowstone (1872)
ID
Grand Teton (1929)
WY
NV
Great Basin (1986)
Capitol Reef (1971)
UT
Zion (1919)
Death Valley (1933)
Bryce Canyon (1928)
Grand Canyon (1919)
AZ
Saguaro (1933)
ND
Theodore Roosevelt (1978)
MN
SD
Wind Cave (1903)
Badlands (1939)
WI
IA
NE
Rocky Mountain (1915)
Arches (1971)
CO
Canyonlands (1964)
Mesa Verde (1906)
Petrified Forest (1962)
NM
Carlsbad Caverns (1930)
Guadalupe Mts. (1972)
TX
MEXICO
KS
MO
IL
OK
AR
LA
Gulf of Mexico
0   125   250 Miles
0   125   250 Kilometers
Albers Equal-Area Projection

Name _____ Date _____

Mountains Around the World

Directions Use the following information to complete the tables below.

- The Rocky Mountains extend about 3,750 miles (6,035 km) through North America. The highest peak of the Rockies, Mount Elbert, in Colorado, is 14,433 feet (4,399 m) tall.
- The Himalayas stretch about 1,550 miles (2,494 km) through Asia. At 29,035 feet (8,850 m), Mount Everest is the tallest peak in the Himalayas, as well as the highest point on Earth.
- The Alps run about 660 miles (1,062 km) through southern Europe. Mont Blanc, on the border of France and Italy, is the highest peak in the Alps at 15,771 feet (4,807 m).
- The Atlas Mountains stretch about 1,200 miles (1,931 km) across northern Africa. Mount Toubkal, in Morocco, is the highest peak in the Atlas Mountains. It is 13,671 feet (4,167 m) tall.
- The Andes Mountains are the longest chain of mountains in the world. They run about 5,500 miles (8,851 km) through South America. At 22,834 feet (6,960 m) tall, Mount Aconcagua, in Argentina, is the highest peak in the Andes.

A. To complete Table A, list the mountain ranges in alphabetical order.

B. To complete Table B, list the mountain ranges in order by length from longest to shortest.

C. To complete Table C, list the mountain ranges in order by the height of their tallest peak from highest to lowest.

TABLE A	TABLE B	TABLE C
Alps	Andes	Himalayas
Andes	Rockies	Andes
Atlas	Himalayas	Alps
Himalayas	Atlas	Rockies
Rockies	Alps	Atlas

© Harcourt

Use after reading Chapter 10, Lesson 3, pages 356–361.

Mountain States

Directions Complete this graphic organizer to make generalizations about mountain regions. Read each set of facts. Then make a generalization based on those facts. Possible responses are given.

Mountain States

FACT 1	+	FACT 2	→	GENERALIZATION
Pioneers used the wide, flat South Pass to cross the Rockies.	+	Pioneers traveled in covered wagons that mules, horses, or oxen could pull over the mountains.	→	Pioneers adapted the way they traveled to the geography of the Rocky Mountains.
Farmers in the Mountain states build their farms in the valleys of the Rockies and on the plains and plateaus east and west of the mountains.	+	Quechuan farmers make terraces to grow their crops on the sides of the Andes Mountains.	→	Farmers must adapt to the land in mountain regions.
People mine gold, silver, lead, copper, and coal from the Rocky Mountains.	+	People mine coal, iron, and salt from the Alps. People mine phosphate, iron, copper, lead, natural gas, and zinc from the Atlas Mountains.	→	People in mountain regions often earn their living mining mineral and metal natural resources.

© Harcourt

Use after reading Chapter 10, pages 340–361.

Name _____   Date _____

10 Test Preparation

Directions Read each question and choose the best answer. Then fill in the circle for the answer you have chosen. Be sure to fill in the circle completely.

1 Which river did Lewis and Clark use to reach present-day North Dakota?
- Ⓐ the Mississippi River
- Ⓑ the Missouri River
- Ⓒ the Columbia River
- Ⓓ the Colorado River

2 Which of the following is *not* a way the Rocky Mountains divide North America?
- Ⓕ They affect the flow of many rivers across the continent.
- Ⓖ They separate the Interior Plains from the Intermountain region.
- Ⓗ They form a natural border between the United States and Canada.
- Ⓙ They separate the Middle West region from the West region of the United States.

3 Which of the following is true about most mountain regions?
- Ⓐ They usually have smaller populations than other kinds of regions.
- Ⓑ Agriculture is the most important industry.
- Ⓒ They usually have more large cities than other kinds of regions.
- Ⓓ The climate is always warm and sunny.

4 Which state is the leading coal producer in the United States?
- Ⓕ Colorado
- Ⓖ Montana
- Ⓗ Utah
- Ⓙ Wyoming

5 Which of the following is *not* an animal that lives naturally in high mountain regions?
- Ⓐ a horse
- Ⓑ a llama
- Ⓒ a bighorn sheep
- Ⓓ a yak

Use after reading Chapter 10, pages 340–361.

Name _____ Date _____

The Southwest Desert Long Ago

One place where the Anasazi built settlements was beneath the towering rock walls of Chaco (CHAH•koh) Canyon, in what is today New Mexico.

Directions Use the time line to answer the questions that follow. The *c.* before a date stands for *circa*, which means "around." Historians use the *c.* when they do not know the exact date.

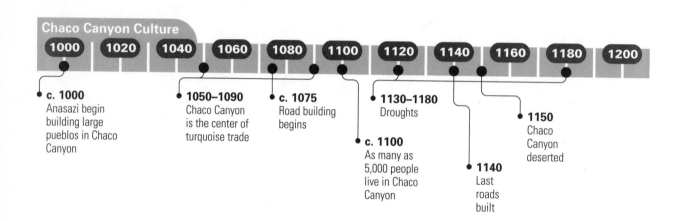

Chaco Canyon Culture

1000 1020 1040 1060 1080 1100 1120 1140 1160 1180 1200

c. 1000
Anasazi begin building large pueblos in Chaco Canyon

1050–1090
Chaco Canyon is the center of turquoise trade

c. 1075
Road building begins

1130–1180
Droughts

c. 1100
As many as 5,000 people live in Chaco Canyon

1140
Last roads built

1150
Chaco Canyon deserted

1. Between what years were Chaco Canyon roads built? from around 1075 to 1140

_____

2. When did the Anasazi begin building pueblos in Chaco Canyon? around 1000

_____

3. In what year did as many as 5,000 people live in the Chaco Canyon community?

around 1100

_____

4. When did the droughts begin in Chaco Canyon? 1130

5. How many decades did the droughts last? five decades

6. By what year had the Anasazi people left Chaco Canyon? 1150

7. About how many years did the Anasazi live in the Chaco Canyon pueblos?

about 150 years

_____

© Harcourt

Use after reading Chapter 11, Lesson 1, pages 366–372.

The Southwest Desert States Today

Directions Use the clues below to solve the crossword puzzle on the next page.

Across

1 This is one of the world's largest reservoirs. It holds the waters of the Colorado River. (2 words)

5 The valleys of the Salt River and the _____ _____ were the first parts of the Arizona desert to be settled. (2 words)

6 a deep gully or ditch carved by running water

7 The _____ Desert covers most of southwestern Arizona.

9 a sudden, heavy rain

10 a person who has no permanent home but keeps moving from place to place

11 Most places in the desert receive _____ only a few times a year.

Down

2 someone who moves from farm to farm with the seasons, harvesting crops (2 words)

3 a supply of water that lies deep beneath Earth's surface

4 The _____ Arizona Project was built to help people use less groundwater.

6 a large pipe or canal built to carry water

8 Native Americans of this culture came to the Sonoran Desert about 2,000 years ago.

Directions After completing the crossword puzzle, copy on the lines below the letters that appear in the shaded boxes.

V   A   O   D   H   O   E   M   R

Directions Now unscramble the letters above to answer this riddle.

What stands as tall as a 54-story building, contains enough concrete to pave a two-lane highway from New York City to San Francisco, and is shown in the drawing on the next page (2 words)?

H   O   O   V   E   R   D   A   M

(continued)

1 L A K E M **2**E A D

3G **4**C

5G I L A R I V E R

6A R R O Y O O N

Q R U T

U A 7**S** O N O R A N R

E N D A

D T **8**H W L

U W O A

9C L O U D B U R S T T T

T K O E

A K R

E

10N O M A D **11**R A I N

Use after reading Chapter 11, Lesson 2, pages 373–379.

READING SKILLS
Predict a Likely Outcome

The following statements provide information about conditions in Grand Canyon National Park.

- More than 5 million people visit the Grand Canyon each year.
- Almost 2 million cars and more than 30,000 tour buses drive into the park each year.
- Glen Canyon Dam changes the amount of water flowing in the Colorado River through the Grand Canyon.
- Many roads, trails, and buildings in the park badly need repairs, which would cost millions of dollars.

Directions **Use the information above to make predictions about Grand Canyon National Park.**

1 **Look at the information you already have about the topic.**
How have humans changed Grand Canyon National Park?

They have built dams, roads, and buildings in the park.

2 **Gather any other information that relates to the topic.**
What do you already know about the Grand Canyon?

Answers will vary but should include information about the park's location and geography. It is located in the Colorado Plateau of northern Arizona, which is mostly arid. Erosion caused by the Colorado River created the canyon over millions of years.

3 **Look for patterns in these events or data.**
How do you think human actions are affecting Grand Canyon National Park?

Answers will vary but should show an understanding that human activity is damaging parts of the park. For example, by building dams, people are changing the natural flow of the Colorado River.

4 **Make a prediction based on any patterns you discover and your own experiences.**
What do you think Grand Canyon National Park might be like in the future?

Answers will vary but should show an understanding of present conditions in the park and how they might affect the park's future. For example, students may say that more people will use the park in the future, possibly causing more damage.

© Harcourt

Deserts of the World

To most people who do not live in desert regions, water seems to be a plentiful resource. However, less than 1 gallon (about 4 L) out of every 100 gallons (379 L) of water on Earth is fresh water that people can use. People all over the world are using enormous amounts of water every day to drink, cook, wash, grow food, and manufacture products. Which parts of the world have enough water and which parts do not? How do people around the world use their water resources?

Directions **Use the map and the graph on page 103 to answer these questions.**

1 Which parts of North America have the least available water?

Mexico and northern Central America, or the southern part of the continent

2 How is most of Earth's fresh water used?

for agriculture

3 Which part of Asia has the most available water?

northern Asia

4 On which continent do people use the most water? the least?

North America; Africa

5 Where on Earth do people use more water for industry than for agriculture?

in Europe

6 Which continent has more available water, Africa or Australia?

Australia

7 Look at the map on page 382 in your textbook. How does the information on that map relate to the information on the map on page 103?

Students' responses should show an understanding of the fact that the places

with the least available water are the major desert regions of the world.

© Harcourt

(continued)

Name _____ Date _____

World Water Usage

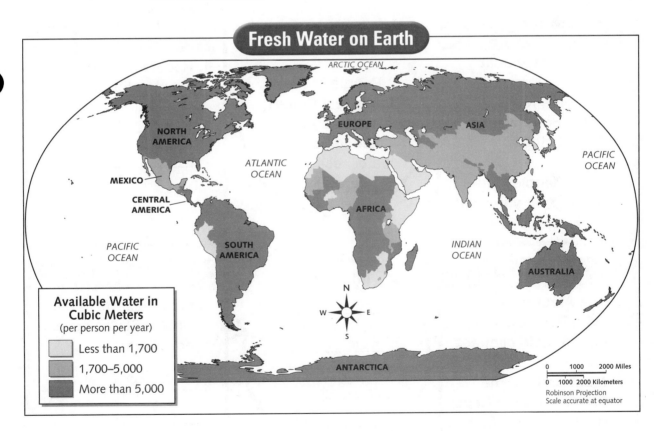

Amount per Year (in cubic meters)

1,300
1,200
1,100
1,000
900
800
700
600
500
400
300
200
100
0

North America · Oceania (Australia and Pacific Islands) · Europe · Asia · South America · Africa

World Region

■ Agriculture ■ Industy ■ Domestic

SOURCE: WHO/UNICEF

Fresh Water on Earth

ARCTIC OCEAN

EUROPE · ASIA · PACIFIC OCEAN

NORTH AMERICA · ATLANTIC OCEAN

MEXICO

CENTRAL AMERICA

PACIFIC OCEAN

SOUTH AMERICA

AFRICA

INDIAN OCEAN

AUSTRALIA

N W E S

ANTARCTICA

0 1000 2000 Miles
0 1000 2000 Kilometers
Robinson Projection
Scale accurate at equator

Available Water in Cubic Meters
(per person per year)

☐ Less than 1,700
☐ 1,700–5,000
☐ More than 5,000

Use after reading Chapter 11, Lesson 3, pages 381–385.

Name _____ Date _____

Southwest Desert States

Directions Complete the following graphic organizer to make inferences about some of the main ideas in the chapter. Read the information that is given. Then fill in the missing statements. Possible responses are given.

SOUTHWEST DESERT STATES

Facts

1. Early peoples in the Southwest Desert region were farmers.

2. They used materials they found around them to build their homes.

Inference

To live in the desert, early peoples of the Southwest Desert region had to adapt to the desert environment. _____

Your Experiences

1. Growing food requires water.

2. Few trees grow in the desert.

Facts

1. People have built _dams_ across rivers to create reservoirs in the Southwest Desert states.

2. Many people land-scape their yards with rocks, cactus, and sand.

Inference

People in the Southwest Desert states try to manage their water resources carefully.

Your Experiences

1. Reservoirs are one way to store water.

2. These landscape items require little or no water.

_____

Facts

1. The Atacama and Gobi Deserts have cool or cold climates.

2. Most parts of the Sahara and the Negev get less than 5 inches (13 cm) of rain each year.

Inference

Deserts around the world have different climates, but they all have scarce water resources. _____

Your Experiences

1. Most deserts in the United States have hot climates.

2. Most places around the world get much more water than that.

© Harcourt

Use after reading Chapter 11, pages 364–385.

Name _____   Date _____

11 Test Preparation

Directions Read each question and choose the best answer. Then fill in the circle for the answer you have chosen. Be sure to fill in the circle completely.

1 Through what desert did Coronado travel while exploring the Southwest Desert region?
   Ⓐ the Sonoran Desert
   Ⓑ the Chihuahuan Desert
   Ⓒ the Great Basin
   Ⓓ the Painted Desert

2 Why did the Anasazi Indians build their homes with adobe?
   Ⓕ because adobe walls were thin
   Ⓖ because few trees grew in the Four Corners' dry climate
   Ⓗ because the tall adobe buildings provided shade for their crops
   Ⓙ because the Anasazi Indians were nomads

3 Which of the following is *not* a natural source of fresh water in deserts?
   Ⓐ cloudbursts
   Ⓑ oases
   Ⓒ reservoirs
   Ⓓ snow

4 Which of the following is *not* a reason why the population of the Southwest Desert states is growing rapidly?
   Ⓕ People have created new sources of water in the region.
   Ⓖ The region has a generally sunny, warm climate.
   Ⓗ People have created a steady supply of electricity in the region.
   Ⓙ Millions of acres in the region are set aside as national parks and forests.

5 Which desert region has a generally cool climate?
   Ⓐ the Atacama Desert
   Ⓑ the Negev
   Ⓒ the North American Desert
   Ⓓ the Sahara

Use after reading Chapter 11, pages 364–385.

Heading to the Pacific

Directions Changes in technology have reduced the amount of time needed to travel from coast to coast in the United States. Use the table below to answer the questions that follow about traveling west over the years.

San Francisco

New York City

Travel Time from Coast to Coast

YEAR	METHOD	TIME
1840	By Wagon	6 Months
1850	By Clipper Ship	3–4 Months
1861	By Train and Stagecoach	26 Days
1869	By Train	7 Days
1932	By Airplane	24 Hours
2000	By Jet	5 Hours

1 What methods of transportation could forty-niners use to reach California during the gold rush? How long did each trip take?

by wagon: 6 months; by clipper ship: 3 to 4 months

2 How much time did it take travelers to go from coast to coast in 1861? How much time did they save after the transcontinental railroad was completed?

26 days; 19 days

3 How much less time does a jet flight across the country take today than an airplane flight did 70 years ago? 19 hours

4 If you were planning to travel from New York City to San Francisco in 1900, which of the transportation methods in the chart would you prefer to use? Why? Accept all answers, excluding airplanes and jets, that students can reasonably defend.

© Harcourt

MAP AND GLOBE SKILLS
Use a Time Zone Map

Directions Use the time zone map below to answer the questions on page 108.

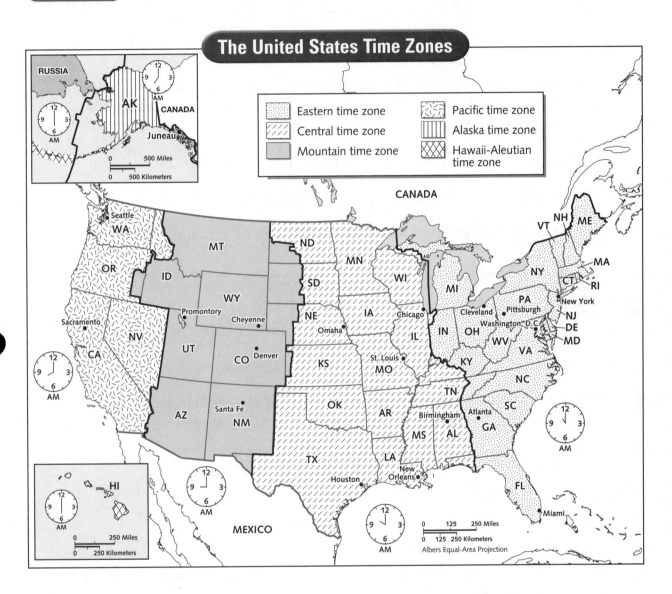

The United States Time Zones

Legend:
- Eastern time zone
- Central time zone
- Mountain time zone
- Pacific time zone
- Alaska time zone
- Hawaii-Aleutian time zone

Albers Equal-Area Projection

(continued)

Name _____ Date _____

1 In which time zone do you live? Answers will vary depending on where students live.

2 When it is 4:00 P.M. in New Mexico, what time is it in

a. Maine? ___6:00 P.M.___   **d.** California? ___3:00 P.M.___

b. Hawaii? ___1:00 P.M.___   **e.** Colorado? ___4:00 P.M.___

c. Minnesota? ___5:00 P.M.___   **f.** Georgia? ___6:00 P.M.___

3 The Union Pacific Railroad built west from Omaha, Nebraska. The Central Pacific Railroad built east from Sacramento, California. The two railroads met at Promontory, Utah, in 1869 to complete the transcontinental railroad.

a. If it is 7:00 P.M. in Sacramento, what time is it in Omaha? ___9:00 P.M.___

b. If it is 8:00 A.M. in Omaha, what time is it in Sacramento? ___6:00 A.M.___

c. If it is 10:00 A.M. in Promontory, what time is it in Omaha? in Sacramento?

11:00 A.M.; 9:00 A.M.

4 Many offices open at 9:00 A.M. and close at 5:00 P.M. If you live in Nevada and you want to call an office in New York, when is the earliest time you could call?

the latest time? 6:00 A.M.; 2:00 P.M. _____

5 Some states are in two different time zones. That means that people in neighboring towns might set their clocks differently! Study the map. Then list five states

that have more than one time zone. Students' answers should come from this list:

Alaska, Florida, Idaho, Indiana, Kansas, Kentucky, Michigan, Nebraska, North

Dakota, Oregon, South Dakota, Tennessee, Texas

6 It is noon in St. Louis, Missouri. Draw hands on the clocks below, showing the correct time for each city.

SEATTLE   PITTSBURGH   JUNEAU   DENVER

Ask students to tell whether each time is A.M. or P.M.

© Harcourt

Land and Climate in the Pacific States

Directions The tables below show average monthly temperatures (in degrees Fahrenheit) and precipitation levels (in inches) for three cities in the Pacific states. Use this information to answer the questions that follow.

ANCHORAGE, ALASKA

	JAN	FEB	MAR	APRIL	MAY	JUNE	JULY	AUG	SEPT	OCT	NOV	DEC
Temperature	15	19	26	36	47	54	58	56	48	35	21	18
Precipitation	0.8	0.8	0.7	0.7	0.7	1.1	1.7	2.4	2.7	2.0	1.1	1.1

SAN DIEGO, CALIFORNIA

	JAN	FEB	MAR	APRIL	MAY	JUNE	JULY	AUG	SEPT	OCT	NOV	DEC
Temperature	57	59	60	62	64	67	71	73	71	68	62	57
Precipitation	1.8	1.5	1.8	0.8	0.2	0.1	0	0.1	0.2	0.4	1.5	1.6

SEATTLE, WASHINGTON

	JAN	FEB	MAR	APRIL	MAY	JUNE	JULY	AUG	SEPT	OCT	NOV	DEC
Temperature	41	44	47	50	56	61	65	66	61	54	46	42
Precipitation	5.4	4.0	3.8	2.5	1.8	1.6	0.9	1.2	1.9	3.3	5.7	6.0

1 Which city is the warmest in December? San Diego _____

2 Which city is the coolest in July? Anchorage _____

3 Which city has the driest climate? the wettest climate? San Diego has the driest climate, and Seattle has the wettest climate. _____

4 How do the locations of Anchorage, Alaska, and San Diego, California, help explain the similarities and differences in their climates? Possible responses: Anchorage has lower temperatures because it is much farther north of the equator than San Diego. They have similar precipitation levels because both cities border the Pacific Ocean and there are no mountains to block moisture from reaching them.

5 Based on climate, in which of these three Pacific cities would you like to live? Explain your answer on a separate sheet of paper. Answers will vary. Look for personal understanding of climate factors in students' explanations of their choices.

© Harcourt

Living in the Pacific States

Directions Each of the following viewpoints was expressed in "A River Dammed," a recent *National Geographic* article about dams built across the Columbia River system. Read the viewpoints. Then answer the questions.

Viewpoint A

"We have taken the Columbia River system beyond the point of balance, and the question now is, do you undo some of this development?"—Michele DeHart

Viewpoint B

"In the old days, we were at the whim of nature here. If we didn't have the rainfall, we couldn't grow our crops. And then we got the water from the dams, and it changed everything."—Bill Watson

Viewpoint C

"Nobody ever said that salmon and dams were made for each other. People needed power. It was a public policy choice."—Dutch Meier

Viewpoint D

"From a biological standpoint, the only way to recover the salmon with any high likelihood of success is to breach [break open] the dams."—Ed Bowles

Viewpoint E

"Fishing is not just a buck for us. It's a way of life. This is a very important part of our culture. . . . And that's all been taken away from us."—Steve Fick

From "Straight Talk" by Rachel Buchholtz in *National Geographic WORLD* Magazine, January/February 2002. Text copyright © 2001 by National Geographic Society. Reprinted by permission of National Geographic Society, 1145 17th Street, N. W., Washington, DC 20036.

1 Which viewpoints contain opinions in favor of the dams? B and C

2 Which viewpoints contain opinions against the dams? A, D, and E

3 Match each of the people below with the viewpoint he or she expressed above:

a biologist _____ D

a potato farmer _____ B

a fisher _____ E

a government leader _____ C

an environmentalist _____ A

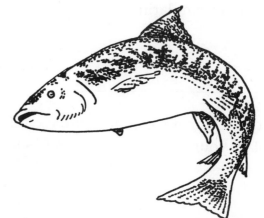

Use after reading Chapter 12, Lesson 3, pages 405–410.

© Harcourt

CITIZENSHIP SKILLS
Act as a Responsible Citizen

Directions One way to act as a responsible citizen is to write a letter to an elected official about an issue that concerns you. First, identify an issue or a problem in your community that interests you. Then, on a separate sheet of paper, use the format below to write a letter describing the issue or problem to a community leader.

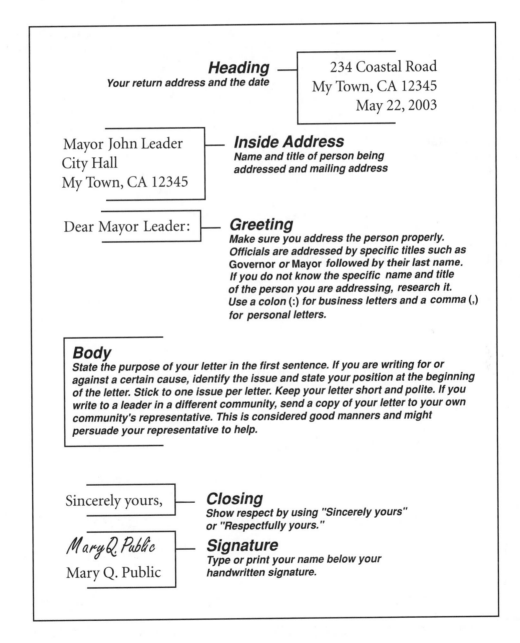

Heading
Your return address and the date

234 Coastal Road
My Town, CA 12345
May 22, 2003

Mayor John Leader
City Hall
My Town, CA 12345

Inside Address
Name and title of person being addressed and mailing address

Dear Mayor Leader:

Greeting
Make sure you address the person properly. Officials are addressed by specific titles such as Governor *or* Mayor *followed by their last name. If you do not know the specific name and title of the person you are addressing, research it. Use a colon (:) for business letters and a* comma (,) *for personal letters.*

Body
State the purpose of your letter in the first sentence. If you are writing for or against a certain cause, identify the issue and state your position at the beginning of the letter. Stick to one issue per letter. Keep your letter short and polite. If you write to a leader in a different community, send a copy of your letter to your own community's representative. This is considered good manners and might persuade your representative to help.

Sincerely yours,

Closing
Show respect by using "Sincerely yours" or "Respectfully yours."

Mary Q. Public
Mary Q. Public

Signature
Type or print your name below your handwritten signature.

Accept letters that follow the format and are well reasoned. Look for aspects of responsible citizenship in the issues described in students' letters.

© Harcourt

Name _____   Date _____

Americans in the Pacific

Directions The seal of a state often contains symbols that tell about the geography, history, and heritage of that state. Study the state seal of Hawaii and the captions that explain it. Then answer the questions that follow.

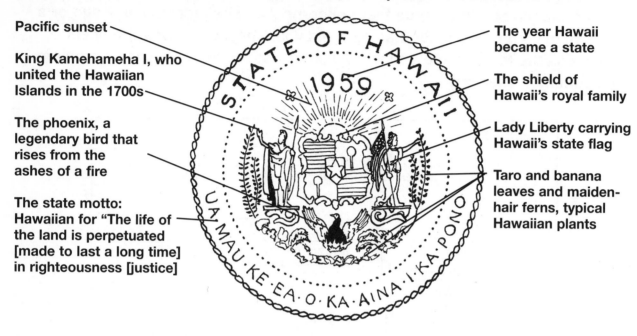

Pacific sunset

King Kamehameha I, who united the Hawaiian Islands in the 1700s

The phoenix, a legendary bird that rises from the ashes of a fire

The state motto: Hawaiian for "The life of the land is perpetuated [made to last a long time] in righteousness [justice]

The year Hawaii became a state

The shield of Hawaii's royal family

Lady Liberty carrying Hawaii's state flag

Taro and banana leaves and maiden-hair ferns, typical Hawaiian plants

1 When did Hawaii become a state? ___1959_____

2 Which parts of the state seal show that Hawaii was once ruled by monarchs?

the portrait of King Kamehameha I and the shield of Hawaii's royal family

3 Why do you think the seal includes a sunset? Possible responses: because of Hawaii's sunny climate; because of Hawaii's western location—the sun sets in the west

4 Why do you think the seal shows a legendary bird rising from fire?

because the islands of Hawaii rose from the ashes of fiery volcanoes

5 What items might you include if you were designing a new state seal for your

state? Answers should reflect the geography, history, and heritage of your state. If

possible, have students share their seals with classmates and family.

Directions On a separate sheet of paper, create a personal seal. Use drawings that tell about your personal history and things that you like to do. Make sure you include your name and a personal motto (some words to live by).

Use after reading Chapter 12, Lesson 4, pages 412–415.

© Harcourt

Oceans Around the World

In 1519 a Portuguese explorer named Ferdinand Magellan sailed from his homeland in search of a water route to Asia. The members of this expedition became the first people to sail around the world.

Directions The map below shows the route that Magellan's ships followed around the world. Use the map to answer the questions that follow.

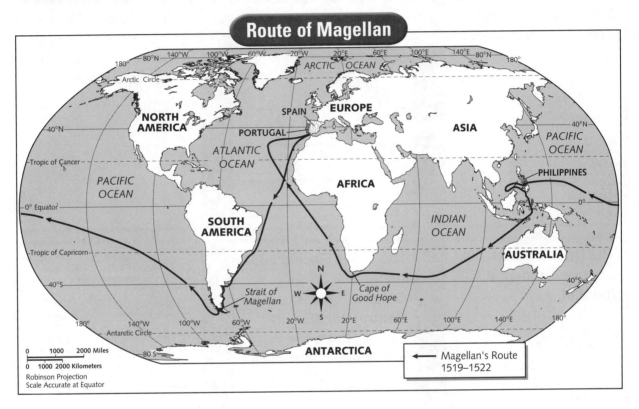

Route of Magellan

1 Where did Magellan begin his voyage? _Portugal_____

2 In which direction did the expedition set sail? _southwest_____

3 At what point did Magellan's ships enter the Pacific Ocean? _after crossing the_ _Strait of Magellan at the tip of South America_____

4 What group of Pacific islands did the ships visit? _the Philippines_____

5 List in order the oceans Magellan's ships sailed. What is the only ocean they did not reach? _Atlantic Ocean, Pacific Ocean, Indian Ocean, Atlantic Ocean; they_ _never reached the Arctic Ocean._____

_____

Use after reading Chapter 12, Lesson 5, pages 416–419.   **Activity Book ▪ 113**

Pacific States

Directions Complete this graphic organizer to predict outcomes of some events that occurred in the Pacific states. Possible responses are given.

PACIFIC STATES

EVENT	FACTS	OUTCOME
Miners discovered gold in California and Alaska.	Many people moved to California and Alaska to look for gold.	California and Alaska gained a large enough population to be able to become states.
The United States built a transcontinental railroad.	The Union Pacific laid tracks west from Omaha, Nebraska. The Central Pacific laid tracks east from Sacramento, California.	Transportation between the East and West coasts was much faster, bringing many more settlers to the Pacific region.
People built dams across rivers in the Pacific states.	More electricity and water for irrigation was available.	The population and economy of the Pacific states grew, but the dams also changed some ecosystems.

Use after reading Chapter 12, pages 388–419.

Name _____ Date _____

12 Test Preparation

Directions Read each question and choose the best answer. Then fill in the circle for the answer you have chosen. Be sure to fill in the circle completely.

1 Between which two mountain ranges does the Willamette Valley lie?
- Ⓐ the Cascade Range and the Sierra Nevada
- Ⓑ the Sierra Nevada and the Coast Ranges
- Ⓒ the Rocky Mountains and the Sierra Nevada
- Ⓓ the Cascade Range and the Coast Ranges

2 In which Pacific state was gold *not* discovered?
- Ⓕ Alaska
- Ⓖ California
- Ⓗ Hawaii
- Ⓙ Washington

3 An earthquake is caused by—
- Ⓐ strong winds and high waves hitting the Pacific coastline.
- Ⓑ the movement and cracking of layers of rock deep inside Earth.
- Ⓒ the rain shadow created by the western mountains.
- Ⓓ an opening in Earth's surface out of which hot gases, ash, and lava pour.

4 Which of the following is *not* a major industry in the Pacific Northwest?
- Ⓕ lumber production
- Ⓖ fishing for salmon and tuna
- Ⓗ drilling for oil and natural gas
- Ⓙ airplane manufacturing

5 Which is the world's largest ocean?
- Ⓐ the Arctic Ocean
- Ⓑ the Atlantic Ocean
- Ⓒ the Indian Ocean
- Ⓓ the Pacific Ocean

Use after reading Chapter 12, pages 388–419.

Name _____ Date _____

Many Places, People, and Ways

Directions Use the information in the table and bar graph below to answer the questions that follow.

People in the United States, 2000	
Ancestry	**Population**
African American	31,606,957
Asian American	10,313,119
European American	190,433,375
Hispanic American	34,334,480
Native American and Native Alaskan American	1,823,395
Native Hawaiian and Pacific Islander American	380,706

SOURCE: U.S. Census Bureau

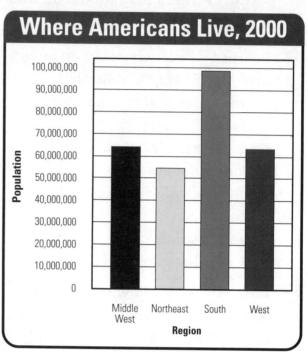

Where Americans Live, 2000

SOURCE: U.S. Census Bureau

1 What is the ancestry of the largest group of people in the United States?

European American

2 In which region of the United States do the most people live? the South

3 How many Asian Americans live in the United States? 10,313,119

4 About how many people live in the Northeast region of the United States?

about 54 million

5 Which two ethnic groups in the United States have about the same number

of people? African Americans and Hispanic Americans

6 Which two regions in the United States have about the same number of people?

the Middle West and the West

© Harcourt

Use after reading Chapter 13, Lesson 1, pages 438–443.

Name _____ Date _____

MAP AND GLOBE SKILLS

Read a Population Map

Directions The size of each state shown on the map below is based on the total population of the state, not on its area, or geographic size. Examine this map, and then compare it with the maps of the United States on pages 428–429 and page 445 in your textbook. Then answer the questions on page 118.

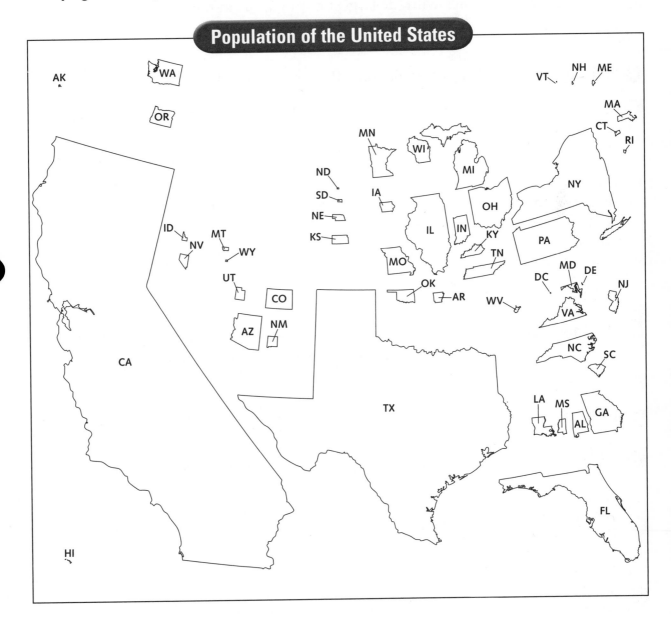

Population of the United States

AK
WA
OR
VT NH ME
MA
CT RI
MN
WI
MI
NY
ND
SD IA
OH
NE
IL IN KY PA
KS
ID MT
NV WY
MO TN
UT OK AR WV DC MD DE NJ
CO VA
AZ NM NC SC
CA
TX LA MS AL GA
HI
FL

(continued)

Use after reading Chapter 13, Skill Lesson, pages 444–445.

© Harcourt

Name _____   Date _____

1 Alaska is the largest state in geographic terms in the United States. Why is it one of the smallest states on the map on page 117?

because Alaska has one of the smallest populations in the United States

2 Why does the map on page 117 show California as the largest state?

because California has the largest population in the United States

3 What are the five states with the largest populations in the United States?

California, Texas, New York, Florida, and Illinois

4 Which state has a larger population—Pennsylvania or Oregon?   Pennsylvania

5 Of the three states Arkansas, Georgia, and Mississippi, which two are the closest in population?   Arkansas and Mississippi

6 Find North Dakota and South Dakota on the map on page 117 and on the map on page 428 in your textbook. What general statement can you make about those states based on their sizes on each map?

North Dakota and South Dakota are two of the largest states in terms of

geographic size, but they have two of the smallest populations.

7 The population of New Mexico is about 2 million. About how many people live in Colorado? How did you use the map on page 117 to answer this question?

about 4 million; On the map on page 117, Colorado is about twice the size of New

Mexico, so Colorado's population is about twice New Mexico's population.

8 How does the map on page 117 compare with the map on page 445 in your

textbook?   Possible responses: Both maps show information about population in

the United States. The map on page 117 shows each state's population, while

the map on page 445 in the textbook shows population density throughout the

United States. The map on page 445 uses different colors to show different pop-

ulation densities, while the map on page 117 uses the sizes of states to show

each state's population.

© Harcourt

A United Country

During the War of 1812, Francis Scott Key stood on the deck of a ship, watching the British fire rockets and bombs at Fort McHenry, which guarded Baltimore, Maryland. At dawn the next day, the American flag still flew over the fort. Key wrote a poem describing the battle and his patriotic feelings. Key's poem was set to music and became very popular. In 1931 the United States government officially declared Key's song the national anthem. It has helped unite Americans ever since.

Directions **Read the first verse of "The Star-Spangled Banner" below. Then follow the instructions at the bottom of the page.**

Encourage students to share their poems or songs with classmates and family. Some students may wish to illustrate their work.

Oh, say can you see by the dawn's early light
What so proudly we hail'd at the twilight's last gleaming,
Whose broad stripes and bright stars through the perilous fight
O'er the ramparts we watch'd were so gallantly streaming?
And the rockets' red glare, the bombs bursting in air,
Gave proof through the night that our flag was still there.
Oh, say does that star-spangled banner yet wave
O'er the land of the free and the home of the brave?

1. Many countries' national anthems celebrate battles and struggles. Underline the words in the first verse of "The Star-Spangled Banner" that describe the Battle of Fort McHenry.

2. The "banner" in the song is the American flag. Circle the words in the verse that describe the American flag.

3. Two words in this verse describe the people of the United States. Find these two words and underline them twice.

4. On a separate sheet of paper, write a short poem or a verse to a song about an experience that has made you feel proud to be an American.

READING SKILLS

Determine Points of View

Directions Read the following statements that some American students recently made about the many different cultures in the United States. Then, on the lines below, describe the points of view you think the students were expressing.

"Some people think that everyone needs to be like them, and that anyone who's different is bad. That's just because those people don't know anything about other cultures."
—Lili, age 10

"In the United States so many people come from so many places that it's really important for everyone to cooperate."
—Aliyeh, age 12

"People are sometimes scared of others who are different from them. But once they get to know them they find out they're not scary—just different."
—Nicholas, age 10

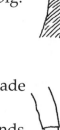

"If someone from a certain culture is not acting very nice, understand that not everyone from that culture acts that way. We shouldn't judge a whole culture by one person. If you are a good person, you are a good person."
—Zaki, age 12

"If people would understand that we're all the same inside, then maybe our differences wouldn't seem so big."
—Ashley, age 12

"One girl at my school was from another country. A lot of people made fun of her because of the way she looked and talked, but I made friends with her. When you get to know people better, you respect them more."
—Maryam, age 11

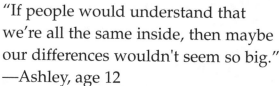

Responses will vary but should explain that all of the statements are about the

importance of understanding other cultures, celebrating and accepting differences,

and judging people individually. Accept all statements that students can reasonably

explain and defend. Encourage students to share their statements with classmates

and family.

Directions On a separate sheet of paper, write a statement to express your point of view about the many different cultures in the United States.

Name _____ Date _____

The United States Economy

People often do work based on the kinds of resources available in their region. The table on the right lists some of the resources, products, or industries of several states. The "Jobs Offered" chart on the left lists different jobs in the United States.

Directions Match each job with the state where it is likely to be offered. Write the letter of the correct state in the box to the left of each job.

Jobs Offered	
h	1. Fisher
i	2. Miner
d	3. Subway car designer
c	4. Paper mill worker
j	5. Cheese maker
f	6. Denim factory worker
g	7. Computer programmer
e	8. Bread maker
b	9. Fruit juice packager
a	10. Oil pipeline builder

State Information	
State	Some Resources, Products, or Industries
a. Alaska	Oil, natural gas
b. Florida	Orange and grapefruit groves
c. Maine	Timber, forestry, pulp
d. Ohio	Transportation equipment, farm machinery
e. North Dakota	Wheat farming
f. South Carolina	Cotton farming
g. Texas	High-tech and aerospace industries
h. Washington	Rivers, ocean ports, fishing
i. West Virginia	Coal, gravel, crushed stone
j. Wisconsin	Dairy farming

Use after reading Chapter 13, Lesson 3, pages 454–459.

Name _____ Date _____

CITIZENSHIP SKILLS
Make Economic Choices

Directions Imagine that you have $20 to spend. Complete the graphic organizer below to help you make an economic choice.

CHOICES
List three $20 items you would like to buy.

Each item selected as a choice by students should have a price of about $20.

OPPORTUNITY COSTS
List the value that each item has to you.

The opportunity cost for each item should reflect what students would have to give up.

ECONOMIC CHOICES

Compare the value of what you will be giving up, or the opportunity cost, for each choice. What are you willing to give up, or trade off? Make an economic choice based on which item will best meet your needs with the $20 you have to spend. List that item below. Your other choices become your opportunity costs.

_____

© Harcourt

Use after reading Chapter 13, Skill Lesson, pages 460–461.

Name _____ Date _____

We the People

Directions Complete this graphic organizer to show that you understand the causes and effects of some important facts about the United States today.

Possible responses are given. **WE THE PEOPLE**

CAUSE	→	EFFECT

People have come from all over the world to live in the United States.		The United States is a diverse country with a great mix of people and cultures.
The warm climate and resources of the Sun Belt have been attracting more people.		**The Sun Belt is one of the fastest-growing regions in the United States.**
The United States government is a democracy.		People in the United States rule by electing leaders to make decisions about the country for them.
Americans learn about one another from the media and computers. They go to school together. They go to many of the same movies and enjoy many of the same sports.		**Americans share a way of life.**
The United States has a free enterprise economy.		People in the United States decide for themselves what kinds of businesses to operate and how they want to run their businesses. People in the United States have many economic choices and opportunities.

© Harcourt

Use after reading Chapter 13, pages 436–461.

13 Test Preparation

Name _____ Date _____

Directions Read each question and choose the best answer. Then fill in the circle for the answer you have chosen. Be sure to fill in the circle completely.

1 From where do most immigrants to the United States now come?

ⓐ Europe

ⓑ Australia

ⓒ South America

ⓓ Latin America

2 Patriotism is—

ⓕ love of one's country.

ⓖ a saying chosen to express the ideals of a group.

ⓗ an unfair feeling of hatred or dislike for a group.

ⓙ something that is built to remind people of the past.

3 Which of the following is *not* a right that all citizens of the United States have?

ⓐ the right to say what they think about the government

ⓑ the right to never pay taxes

ⓒ the right to worship as they please

ⓓ the right to have a fair trial

4 What is the goal of nearly every business?

ⓕ to loan and borrow money

ⓖ to buy goods and sell them directly to consumers

ⓗ to make a profit

ⓙ to organize, share, and use information

5 The United States takes part in the global economy by—

ⓐ trading goods and services with different countries.

ⓑ producing computers and using the Internet.

ⓒ buying large amounts of goods from producers and selling them to other businesses.

ⓓ studying and managing its methods of production.

© Harcourt

Use after reading Chapter 13, pages 436–461.

A Plan of Government

The Constitution of the United States begins with the Preamble, or introduction. The Preamble tells why the Constitution was written. It explains that the writers wanted to set up a fair form of government and make sure of certain freedoms—for themselves and for future American citizens.

Directions **Read the Preamble of the United States Constitution below. Then figure out what the numbered lines mean. Write each number next to the line's best explanation.**

We the people of the United States,
in order to form a more perfect Union,[1]
establish justice,
insure domestic tranquility,[2]
provide for the common defense,
promote the general welfare,[3]
and secure the blessings of liberty
to ourselves and our posterity,[4]
do ordain and establish[5]
this Constitution for the United States of America.

A. ___2___ make sure there is peace at home

B. ___4___ to everyone belonging to this country and all who later become part of this country

C. ___5___ make official and set up

D. ___3___ encourage health, happiness, and comfort

E. ___1___ to make a better, single government

Name _____   Date _____

CHART AND GRAPH SKILLS
Read a Flow Chart

Directions The flow chart below shows some of the powers of each branch of the federal government and how the system of checks and balances applies to each branch. Use the flow chart to answer the questions that follow.

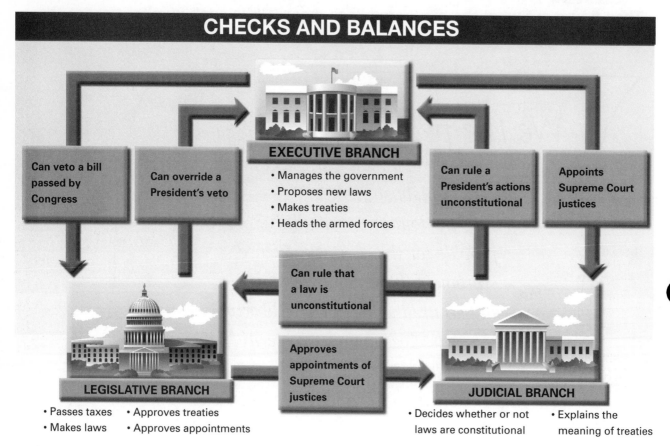

CHECKS AND BALANCES

EXECUTIVE BRANCH
• Manages the government
• Proposes new laws
• Makes treaties
• Heads the armed forces

Can veto a bill passed by Congress

Can override a President's veto

Can rule a President's actions unconstitutional

Appoints Supreme Court justices

Can rule that a law is unconstitutional

Approves appointments of Supreme Court justices

LEGISLATIVE BRANCH
• Passes taxes   • Approves treaties
• Makes laws   • Approves appointments

JUDICIAL BRANCH
• Decides whether or not   • Explains the
  laws are constitutional   meaning of treaties

1 According to the flow chart, how does each branch of the federal government affect laws in the United States? The executive branch proposes new laws, the legislative branch makes new laws, and the judicial branch decides whether laws are constitutional.

2 How are vetoes an important part of the checks and balances system in the federal government? The executive branch can veto a bill passed by Congress, thus checking the power of the legislative branch. In turn, the legislative branch can override a President's veto, thus checking the power of the executive branch.

Use after reading Chapter 14, Skill Lesson, pages 474–475.

Levels of Government

Directions Complete the three charts below by filling in the correct information for each level of government in the United States. Describe each branch in each level of government, each level's main job, and some of the services each level provides. If you need help, reread Chapter 14, Lesson 2, in your textbook.

FEDERAL GOVERNMENT	
Executive Branch	the President
Legislative Branch	Congress
Judicial Branch	federal courts (including the Supreme Court)
Main Job	to take care of issues and problems that affect the entire country
Some Services It Provides	Possible responses: oversees the military; prints and coins money; oversees the postal service; supports national parks; builds and repairs interstate highways

STATE GOVERNMENTS	
Executive Branch	the governor
Legislative Branch	state legislature
Judicial Branch	state courts
Main Job	to take care of issues and problems that affect the state
Some Services They Provide	Possible responses: build and manage state highways and parks; oversee state schools; help people in the state get food, shelter, and health care

LOCAL GOVERNMENTS	
Executive Branch	board of county commissioners, the mayor or the city manager
Legislative Branch	board of county commissioners, city council
Judicial Branch	county and city courts
Main Job	to take care of issues and problems that affect the specific community
Some Services They Provide	Possible responses: provide police and fire protection; manage garbage collection and public utilities; build and repair county and city roads and streets; run local schools, libraries, and parks

© Harcourt

United States Citizenship

Directions The declaration below was written in 1913 by the National Child Labor Committee, an organization that worked to outlaw child labor. At that time thousands of young people in the United States did not go to school. Instead, they worked long hours both day and night in factories, mines, and other industries. Read the declaration. Then answer the questions on page 129.

Declaration of Dependency by the Children of America in Mines and Factories and Workshops Assembled

WHEREAS, We, Children of America, are declared to have been born free and equal, and

WHEREAS, We are yet in bondage [slavery] in this land of the free; are forced to toil the long day or the long night, with no control over the conditions of labor, as to health or safety or hours or wages, and with no right to the rewards of our service, therefore be it

RESOLVED, I—That childhood is endowed with [granted] certain inherent [natural] and inalienable rights, among which are freedom from toil for daily bread; the right to play and to dream; the right to the normal sleep of the night season; the right to an education, that we may have equality of opportunity for developing all that there is in us of mind and heart.

RESOLVED, II—That we declare ourselves to be helpless and dependent; that we are and of right ought to be dependent, and that we hereby present the appeal of our helplessness that we may be protected in the enjoyment of the rights of childhood.

RESOLVED, III—That we demand the restoration of our rights by the abolition [ending] of child labor in America.

Alexander J. McKelway, 1913

(continued)

1 For whom did the National Child Labor Committee claim to speak?

for all children of America

2 What demand does the declaration make?

to abolish, or end, child labor in America

3 According to the declaration, what hardships did child workers face during the early 1900s in the United States?

Children were forced to work long hours day and night, with no control over their

health, safety, hours, or wages.

4 According to the declaration, with what rights are all children born?

freedom from having to work for their food; the right to play and to dream; the

right to sleep at night; and the right to an education and equal opportunities

Directions **Complete the chart below by listing five rights that you think all young people in the United States should have. For each right, describe why you feel that right is important and what you think your responsibility is concerning that right.**

RIGHTS OF YOUNG AMERICANS	
What do you think is your right?	**Why is each right important? What is your responsibility?**
1.	Accept all rights that are reasonable and that
2.	students can justify as important. Students
3.	should show an understanding of the
4.	relationship between rights and
5.	responsibilities in their responses.

© Harcourt

Use after reading Chapter 14, Lesson 3, pages 482–487.

The United States and the World

After World War II ended in 1945, the United States government started a program to involve private citizens in world affairs. By helping individuals around the world form personal relationships, the government hoped to lessen the chance of future world conflicts. Today the program the government started is called Sister Cities International. It helps communities in the United States form special partnerships with communities around the world to increase global cooperation and understanding.

Directions The table below lists the largest city in each of the four major regions of the United States and some of their sister cities. Find the city located in the region where you live, and choose one of its sister cities that you think is interesting. Then, on a separate sheet of paper, write a letter to a fourth grader living in that sister city. Explain the location of your city relative to the sister city's. Describe your region's geography, economy, and history. Share what you like about living where you do and tell about things you do for fun. Finally, explain how you think writing a personal letter like this can help form good relations among people and countries around the world.

UNITED STATES CITY	SISTER CITIES AROUND THE WORLD
Chicago, Illinois	Moscow, Russia; Paris, France; Toronto, Canada
Houston, Texas	Istanbul, Turkey; Perth, Australia; Shenzhen, China
Los Angeles, California	Athens, Greece; Berlin, Germany; Mexico City, Mexico
New York City, New York	Cairo, Egypt; Rome, Italy; Tokyo, Japan

Students should correctly identify the largest city in their region of the United States and should choose one of that city's sister cities around the world. In their letters students should describe the location of their city relative to the sister city's, and their region's geography, economy, and history. Encourage students to share their letters with classmates.

Use after reading Chapter 14, Lesson 4, pages 488–491.

© Harcourt

Name _____   Date _____

Our Country's Government

Directions Complete this graphic organizer by describing different points of view expressed in this chapter. Possible responses are given.

OUR COUNTRY'S GOVERNMENT

GOVERNMENT

		Details		Point of View
"Governments are instituted among Men, deriving their just Powers from the Consent of the Governed." —*President Thomas Jefferson*	→	derive power from the governed	→	Jefferson believes that the government's power to rule is given by the people.

CIVIL RIGHTS

		Details		Point of View
"I have a dream that my four little children will one day live in a nation where they will not be judged by the color of their skin, but by the content of their character." —*Dr. Martin Luther King, Jr.*	→	dream for the future: stop prejudice; equality for all	→	King believes that all people should be judged by their character rather than their background.

WORLD AFFAIRS

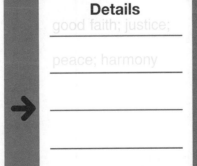

		Details		Point of View
"Observe good faith and justice toward all nations. Cultivate peace and harmony with all." —*President George Washington*	→	good faith; justice; peace; harmony	→	Washington is giving advice on the future role of the United States in world affairs—stressing fairness and peace.

Use after reading Chapter 14, pages 464–491.

Name _____ Date _____

14 Test Preparation

Directions Read each question and choose the best answer. Then fill in the circle for the answer you have chosen. Be sure to fill in the circle completely.

1 What document explains how our federal government works?
- Ⓐ the Declaration of Independence
- Ⓑ the Constitution of the United States
- Ⓒ the Emancipation Proclamation
- Ⓓ the Bill of Rights

2 Who makes sure that laws in the United States are applied fairly?
- Ⓕ the Supreme Court
- Ⓖ the House of Representatives
- Ⓗ the Senate
- Ⓙ the President of the United States

3 Which level of government prints and coins money in the United States?
- Ⓐ the federal government
- Ⓑ the state governments
- Ⓒ the county governments
- Ⓓ the city governments

4 The Civil Rights movement worked to—
- Ⓕ reduce taxes and balance the national budget.
- Ⓖ ensure the rights of citizens to equal treatment under the law.
- Ⓗ provide money, goods, and services for countries in need.
- Ⓙ form alliances to solve international problems.

5 Why does the United States often provide foreign aid?
- Ⓐ to fund international scientific projects
- Ⓑ to protect Earth's environment
- Ⓒ to help countries reach peaceful agreements to conflicts
- Ⓓ to address the world's problems of poverty, hunger, and disease

© Harcourt

Use after reading Chapter 14, pages 464–491.